Communication Skills for Working with Children and Young People

Communication Skills for Working with Children and Young People

Introducing Social Pedagogy

Third Edition

Pat Petrie

Jessica Kingsley *Publishers*
London and Philadelphia

First published in 1989 by Arnold as *Communicating with Children and Adults: Interpersonal Skills for Those Working with Babies and Children*
Second edition published in 1997 by Arnold as *Communicating with Children and Infants: Interpersonal Skills for Early Years and Playwork*

This third edition published in 2011
by Jessica Kingsley Publishers
116 Pentonville Road
London N1 9JB, UK
and
400 Market Street, Suite 400
Philadelphia, PA 19106, USA

www.jkp.com

Copyright © Pat Petrie 1989, 1997, 2011
Illustrations copyright © Harry Venning 1997, 2011
Printed digitally since 2013

Library of Congress Cataloging in Publication Data
A CIP catalog record for this book is available from the Library of Congress

British Library Cataloguing in Publication Data
A CIP catalogue record for this book is available from the British Library

ISBN 978 1 84905 137 8
eISBN 978 0 85700 331 7

Contents

Acknowledgements

Many different professionals who work with children and young people have let me see them at work and discussed their work with me. Their experience has helped inform *Communication Skills for Working with Children and Young People* and I am most grateful to them. I am also grateful to the late Rachel Pinney for letting me observe Children's Hours, and Jane Lane and Bob Hughes for their advice. I especially acknowledge the National Nursery Examination Board (NNEB) which first supported my work developing interpersonal skills training and the Departments of Health and of Education which funded my research into social pedagogy. None of the above are responsible for any errors of judgement the book may contain.

Introduction

This third edition of *Communication Skills for Working with Children and Young People* is for people who work with or intend to work with children and young people across the age range from babies to teenagers. It is relevant to work in many different settings from nurseries to childminding, adventure playgrounds, after-school clubs, holiday playschemes, fostering and residential care – and others. It enlarges on the second edition by bringing together ideas derived from social pedagogy and more guidance on interpersonal communication. Both apply to work with adults, young people and children and both are deeply concerned with humans as social beings and the relationships between them. Forming relationships is the central process in working with children and young people. The work is first and foremost *personal*.

The book does not cover written communications, important though these are.

Social pedagogy

To many English speakers, the term 'pedagogy' sounds unfamiliar and many are put off by what sounds like quite an academic term. But we have many words that end in 'ogy' where the *g* has a soft sound – think of 'psychology' and 'geology'. In England, the term 'pedagogy' is mainly applied to schooling and formal education, while *social* pedagogy has been little known until fairly recently. But in mainland Europe both terms are applied to a broad set of services such as those listed above.

It is sometimes said that social pedagogy is where care and education meet, relating to support for children's development, overall. To put it another way, social pedagogy is about bringing up children, it is 'education' in the broadest sense of that word and is concerned with the whole child: a physical, thinking, feeling, creative human being, in relationship with other people and already contributing to our society.

In various research studies, undertaken by myself and colleagues at the Institute of Education, European colleagues have explained social pedagogy in the following ways: It's where care and education meet... It's nurturing children... It's about seeing children as social beings and supporting them in their social relationships... It's upbringing and supporting the child's development: education in its broadest sense.

Parents are sometimes referred to as a child's 'first pedagogues', the people who are first involved in bringing the child up. The expression describes what parents do apparently instinctively. This is a helpful idea but it needs enlarging. Social pedagogy is a professional occupation; it is not parenting and its demands require more than instinct or the sort of unspoken knowledge that people often rely on in their private lives. Social pedagogues require certain professional understandings, attitudes and skills before they can involve themselves in bringing up children as whole persons. In mainland Europe, social pedagogy can be studied at degree and higher degree level. In this book, I will touch on areas of social pedagogy which are relevant for interpersonal communication. For many people, this will be a first introduction to the subject. Suggestions for more advanced reading are given in the Bibliography at the end of the book.

I hope that as you work through the book it will become clear that communicating well is not an end in itself. In social pedagogy, it is necessary to communicate well in order to achieve aims that arise from distinctive values and understandings; social pedagogy is based on values: it is an ethical practice, not a technique. Here are some of its values:

Pedagogues often speak about their work as involving the head, hand and heart:

- *The heart*: they bring their hearts to their work as ethical and emotional beings. They are aware of their own emotional reactions to the work and how these can affect their relationships and communications with children and others. They treat others with respect, valuing their contributions to life together. Through the relationships they form with the children and adults they work with, they aim to build security, trust and self-esteem. They can empathise with other people, understand how they are feeling, trying to see their point of view and knowing that this will often be different from their own – they sometimes speak of this as different people having different 'life worlds'.

- *The hands*: pedagogues see their work as practical. Relationships are formed in the course of everyday practical, ordinary activities such as preparing food or taking children to school.

- *The head*: pedagogues are reflective practitioners, open to learning about relevant theory, assessing their work in the light of understandings and self-knowledge and on this basis, taking decisions about how best to take the work forward, according to the best interests of children and young people.

Social pedagogues see themselves as sharing the same 'living space' as the people they work with. They try to get away from feelings of 'us and them' between different professionals and between adults and children, ensuring that, whatever the setting, a group values all its members. There is an understanding that everyone present contributes to group life and to decisions about activities, and affects the emotional climate. In the 'living space' all group members are equal persons, with a right to participate and be heard. Pedagogues work 'in dialogue' with children and colleagues, believing that different perspectives make for richness and creativity.

Sometimes social pedagogues speak about the 'three Ps', the professional, the personal and the private. As professionals they are aware of their responsibilities towards others and they bring professional knowledge, skills and attitudes to their work. At the same time, they see themselves as persons: fellow human beings with colleagues and children, not afraid to express feelings, or talk about their lives or share humour and fun. But they also judge which matters are private and should remain so, deciding what is for sharing and what would be inappropriate to share.

Social pedagogues value teamwork and the contribution of other people in bringing up children and young people. So they try to form good working relationships with other professionals and members of the local community, and especially with parents and carers.

In all aspects of their profession, social pedagogues are aware of being role models for the adults and children they work with, especially in the respect they show to others, their attentive listening and supportive responses to other group members.

So why is this relevant for your work? All of the above values and understandings underpin the interpersonal skills which are presented in this book. The book is about communicating with not just children but also adults – whether they be colleagues, parents of the child, or others – using the same practical, theoretical and ethical framework for all interpersonal exchanges and relationships.

People working with children and young people need to be able to communicate effectively with everyone they meet professionally. (We will look at what is meant by 'effectively' in Chapter 1.) Directly or indirectly, practitioners' communications affect the children and young people they work with. It is in their interests that all the adults concerned should be able to communicate and co-operate as well as they can; staff who are trained in interpersonal skills can take a lead in this.

Communication Skills for Working with Children and Young People shows ways in which staff can take responsibility for their own part in any act of communication and at the same time support the other person, child or adult, to communicate effectively.

The book's overall aims are that the reader should:

- be introduced to some of the ideas and values of social pedagogy and how these relate to interpersonal communication
- become aware of the central place of relationships and interpersonal communication in their work
- come to an understanding that effective interpersonal communication depends on skills that can be acquired
- learn to communicate in ways which serve the best interests of children and young people and show respect for the people they work with, based on an understanding that people are of equal worth.

Chapter 1 is an introduction to the subject; it discusses interpersonal communication in general, what 'effective' communication aims at in social pedagogy, and what is meant by verbal and non-verbal communication.

Chapter 2 is about an interpersonal approach with babies and preverbal communication, that is communication before the child acquires language.

Chapters 3 to 6 are a sequence about listening – a core skill for people who work with children and young people and look at how practitioners' supportive listening and responding builds respectful relationships. Careful listening is one of the ways in which practitioners can come to understand other people's perspectives, their 'life world'.

Chapter 7 looks at self-disclosure: personal communications about oneself and when this is helpful in the work situation and when it is inappropriate.

Chapter 8 focuses on different types of questions and their uses; it also examines adults' questions addressed to children as well as children's questioning of adults; it gives examples of entering dialogue with a child and what a rich experience this can be.

Chapter 9 is about social control through interpersonal communications, including 'blaming' behaviour and ways in which some groups of people are not given equal value as fellow human beings, with discussion and exercises on communications involving sexism, racism and disablism.

Chapters 10 and 11 present ways of communicating in a constructive manner in situations where there is conflict, including how to approach other people – across the age range – about behaviour which is unacceptable and how to receive criticism from other people. In social pedagogy, situations involving conflict are seen as sources of creativity, new understandings and better relationships when they are handled skilfully and with respect. These chapters draw on what has been learned in Chapters 3 to 6.

Chapter 12 gives advice about working in meetings. It can be applied to staff meetings and parents' groups, or meetings for young people. It looks at being an effective group member and at setting up and leading a group. The chapter draws on much that has been learned earlier in the book.

Chapter 13 considers the subject of confidentiality. It stresses the importance of professionalism, of not divulging personal information about children and their families, but also discusses situations where it is essential to let senior staff know about serious concerns about a child or young person.

Chapter 14 briefly draws together all the main themes of the book and it is followed by a list of books and other readings to take students' understanding of social pedagogy and of interpersonal communication further.

Exercises and observations

Communication Skills for Working with Children and Young People contains many exercises, including suggestions for observations and materials for discussion. The discussion material is headed 'Reflection: things to discuss or think about', to suggest that if you are not taking part in a course with fellow students, you can still take time to reflect on the case studies which are presented and the questions which are posed. Where the book is being used on a course, discussion can take place in small groups or the whole class can take part together. Some tutors may wish to use the discussion points as the basis of written work.

Any exercises or observations undertaken between training sessions can be usefully discussed by all students at the next session. Comparing experiences can lead to further understanding of what aids effective, ethical interactions and what hinders them.

Observations

There are many suggestions for observations in this book. Some suggestions are for carrying out observations at your work place, or in your training placement. Others are for observations which you can carry out at home or elsewhere. In some chapters it is suggested that the student watches television for the purpose of observing interpersonal communication. It would be possible for a class tutor to record short excerpts from a television drama for observation and discussion by the whole class.

Observing is a useful way of learning about behaviour, including how people communicate together (Fawcett 2009). Carrying out an observation is not the same as just casually watching what is happening, it means watching in such a way that you learn all you can from a situation. There are two main sorts of suggestions for observation made in the book, formal and less formal. A more formal observation is one in which you make an arrangement to carry out the observation, for example in a play centre, a nursery or with a mother and child, and then carry it out, over a set period of time and at the same time making a written record of your observations.

Formal observations

If you are observing interpersonal communication formally, there are certain steps to be taken in advance, which you should discuss with your tutor. Write a letter for the different people involved explaining the reasons for carrying out the observation (you are studying interpersonal communication), what will be involved (you will observe and take notes), and that what you observe will be treated as confidential to be discussed only with fellow students as part of your course, and without divulging names. Obtain written consent to carry out the observation. If the people involved are children and young people they and their carers should give consent to the observation.

From the outset be very clear about the sort of communication on which you will concentrate. Before you start, copy out the aims of the observation according to the suggestions included throughout the book and state what you are going to look out for.

It is sometimes a good idea to just watch for ten minutes, before you start to observe properly. During this time if any children approach you and try to get you talking or show you things, tell them in a friendly way that today you cannot talk because you are going to be busy writing. They will soon understand and leave you free to observe. During this time you can make some notes describing the background to the observation, for example: the sort of room you are in, how many children are present, their age range, the number of staff present and what activities are going on. This gives a context for your observation.

If the observation is to be of several children, observe each one for several minutes in turn. This child is known as the target child. Do not let your attention wander from one child to another. Make notes about each episode of communication as it happens, then return to observing. Devise your own shorthand for your notes, in advance. For example call the child you are observing *X* (and other children who approach the observation child *A, B, C,* and so on. Identify any adults involved by a number: *1, 2, 3.* Use *pl* for play and *gv* for gives, *t* for touches, *sm* for smiles, and so on. Do not have too many abbreviations or you will forget them. Write down a short list of those you are going to use in advance. Try to be as factual as you can be in your observation, say what is happening, don't give your opinion about it; so write 'The baby is crying loudly' not 'The baby is making a terrible noise.'

The same method can be used when observing television programmes (later in the book there are some suggestions about observing interpersonal communication which takes place in television programmes). You will have to be ready to switch attention from one character to another if there is a change of scene. You will not know this in advance.

If you have the opportunity, carry out the same observation exercise more than once. This gives you useful practice.

Less formal observations

Some of the suggestions in the book are for less formal observations, for example the observations in a public place like a station or park playground. On such occasions, because it may be difficult to write down your observations there and then, you should write notes about what you noticed as soon as possible after the event. You can write them up more fully later. In some chapters there are suggestions about being aware of specific types of communication as they happen around you, at work or in everyday life: the use of questions, for example, or how adults respond to children. Clearly it is not possible to write notes about these episodes, which have not been planned, as you would for an observation which had been arranged in advance. In many circumstances it would not be acceptable to take out a pen and make notes, there and then. Nevertheless it is useful to write a description of the people involved, how the interaction progressed and any outcome that you were aware of. The important thing is to become alert to how people communicate.

Confidentiality

It is very important that people should not be identifiable from anything you write as a result of your observations. Do not use people's names in case a third party comes across your notes and can identify those concerned. This includes children's names and adults' names; it also includes the name of the service where you have been observing.

CHAPTER 1

Interpersonal Communication and Social Pedagogy

This first chapter is going to explain what is meant by interpersonal communication and introduce some of the ways in which people communicate in person. It will also begin to look at how social pedagogy and interpersonal communication connect. Working with people is fascinating, rewarding and challenging and requires good interpersonal communication skills. Throughout the book I will take for granted that readers want to be professionally effective in the way they communicate with those they work with: babies, children, parents, young people, colleagues and others.

Research has shown that it is perfectly possible for people to improve their communication skills, and I hope that this book will help readers to do so. But that is not the whole picture. We will first consider what effective interpersonal communication means: it is much more than speaking clearly and fluently. An effective practitioner has also identified their professional aims and they interact with other people in ways that helps them to achieve these. An ineffective practitioner may know what they want to achieve but the way in which they relate to other people gets in the way. Some people may have thought very little about their professional aims – in which case they cannot possibly be effective.

Communicating with other people, face to face, is an activity which is satisfying, interesting and sometimes very demanding. It is the central process in settings such as nurseries, residential care, foster care, and play services. It is work that is first and foremost personal and should be seen as being conducted primarily for the sake of all the children, young people and/or adults who use the services: it is value-based.

Professional aims are always based on values – although individual practitioners may not always be aware of this. By values I mean the principles that are taken to be most important, such as democracy, equality and respect for other people. These are some of the values of social pedagogy, part of its ethical basis. They are the underlying messages that may not be put into words but which are conveyed in how social pedagogues communicate with other people. These messages are effective because they help fulfil the aims of social pedagogy. They let people know, among other things, that they are valued and will be treated fairly and there will be many examples of this, throughout the book.

Interpersonal communication

Interpersonal communication takes place when people of whatever age interact. They talk, listen, observe and react to each other, exchanging many sorts of information, in many different ways. They are present to each other. Communication is the very stuff of social life. From babyhood on, we let other people know about ourselves, our needs, feelings and ideas – and we learn about them. The content of our communications is as varied as life itself, from our angry cries as frustrated toddlers to the words of encouragement and support given to young people in foster or residential care. Similarly, other people, whether they are children or adults, communicate their experience, their feelings and their knowledge to us.

A simple way of thinking about interpersonal communication is as messages, or information, which we send out to other people and messages we receive from them. So a toddler who points insistently towards a dog and says 'daw...daw...' is sending a message about something that has caught his attention. He may look towards you (another message) to check that you see what he sees. If you receive his message you may give him an answering message – a smile, a nod or some words: 'Yes, it's a dog.'

A ten-year-old taps on your arm to get your attention and without a word, but with great delight, holds up a completed model, the paint still wet, for your attention. Without words she conveys pride in her achievement and confidence that you will understand and share that pride.

A 13-year-old, newly arrived in a residential home, speaks in a low voice, uses few words, does not make eye contact and sits with hunched shoulders. It looks as though he doesn't want to communicate but this is a powerful message in itself. In spite of himself, he is communicating.

As human beings we are sophisticated in our communications, using our faces, bodies and voices for sending messages to other people. We use our senses of sight, hearing and touch for receiving messages, all backed up by our experience of human communication, so that we make sense of incoming messages, and organise and co-ordinate outgoing ones. Mostly, we are hardly aware of the complexity of what we're doing when we are with other people. Communication is an exchange and there are always at least two people engaged in it. Imagine someone singing in the bathroom or a child smiling in a hiding place where no one can see her; however great the singing or expressive the smile, these two people are not communicating – because no one is listening to the singer and no one observes that the child is happy.

In the past, a popular saying in working with very young children was 'bathe the child with language' (and certainly it's necessary for children to hear language in order to speak and understand) but flooding children with language is not the same as communicating effectively with them. If they don't understand, or don't want to listen, the message you wanted to communicate is blocked. Similarly there is more to communicating with the adults you meet at work, than simply telling them something. Unless they take part by listening there is no communication, or the communication you intended can be distorted.

Communication takes place when someone sends a message and the other person receives it. It is a two-way process. You play your part in communication by listening to and being attentive to other people, as well as by talking to them. Listening carefully to another person, being sensitive to their feelings and to their point of view, is a way of respecting them and being open to their communications.

Messgaes pass from one person to another through touch, sounds, gestures and expressions as well as words

For social pedagogues this way of working is essential. It is one of the bases on which trusting relationships can be built. Social pedagogues often think about communication in terms of dialogue: the way in which people build meaning together. Communication, as we shall see, is not just a matter of giving information and asking questions; sensitive listening plays a large part.

OBSERVATION

☐ Spend half an hour observing interpersonal communication in some place where adults and children are together. It could be a nursery, a kids club, a park sand-pit, or a playground.

☐ Become aware of who starts any communication between adults and children – the adult or the child?

☐ How do people communicate without words? How many different ways do you notice?

☐ Do the communications seem to be successful – do people get through to one another – or not?

☐ What discoveries do you make?

Non-verbal communication

After doing the observation you may have become more aware of the means children and adults use for communicating. Verbal communication, how we speak, is important but there are other ways of letting people know what we think and what we feel, used even more frequently than words. Communication which does not depend on words is called non-verbal communication.

People convey messages non-verbally by using their:

• voices

• faces

• bodies.

Voices communicate

The way that people speak has an effect on the meaning of the words they use. Experiment saying the phrase 'Would you like to go swimming?' to convey different messages to the other person, such as:

• I like doing things with you…

• I feel bored…

• I don't think you heard me the first time…

• I'm in a hurry…

You will find that the same words can carry very different meanings according to how someone uses his or her voice.

Become aware of some of the following when you are listening to people:

- The speed at which they speak: fast, slow, speeding up, slowing down.
- How they pause or hesitate in what they say.
- The volume: loud, shouting, moderate, very quiet, whispering, inaudible.
- The pitch of the voice: high, screeching, low, middle register.
- Inflection: how the voice rises and falls.
- The emphasis or stress they give to certain words.

Meaningful sounds

People of all ages make wordless sounds to convey messages to other people. These include: sighs, squeals, laughs, moans, yawns and cries. Sometimes, children are less inhibited than adults in using their voices like this. Imagine a moment of great excitement with teenagers playing in a swimming pool, or of conflict between toddlers over a toy. But also think of adults at a football match, or seeing a new baby for the first time. These are all occasions when people often use their voices to express feelings, but without using words.

Being sensitive to voices

Someone who is sensitive to how people use their voices is in touch with a great deal of information about how other people are feeling.

For example you know just by the quality of a baby's squeals of laughter, that he is no longer happily excited with a rough-and-tumble game but is on the verge of becoming anxious. So you quieten the game down and reassure him.

You are talking to a mother about an outing planned during the summer. The mother replies quietly, slowly and hesitantly, using little emphasis. You realise that she sounds depressed, and take this into account in how you respond to her. You think that this is probably not the right moment to overload her with information about the outing.

OBSERVATION

☐ Watch a play or soap opera on television and for quarter of an hour pay special attention to one main character and how they use their voice.

☐ Notice the speed, pauses, volume, pitch and inflection with which the person speaks.

☐ What is communicated to other people by the way in which the actor uses his or her voice?

Faces communicate

Whether we intend it or not, our faces can convey a great deal of meaning. Some people seem to control their expressions and look disconcertingly 'dead pan'. Others have very mobile faces, showing fleeting thoughts and emotions clearly. Every day you see a range of expressions when you are at work, on the faces of staff, volunteers, parents and children. What do you think the various expressions that you encounter mean? Is it easy to interpret them?

Smiling, gazing and frowning are all common and important ways of communicating, making use of the face.

Smiling

Smiling needs no explanation; it's something we have all done from the time we were a few months old and the messages communicated by a smile are, for the most part, clear: 'I'm happy...pleased...friendly...' These are positive, warm messages. We also recognise an insincere smile when we see it. This comes from the head rather than the heart, and involves the mouth but – sometimes chillingly – not the eyes.

Gazing

Gazing means looking directly into the face of another person, perhaps gazing into their eyes. People use gaze unselfconsciously; for example you usually look towards someone who is speaking, if you are interested in what they have to say; turning your gaze away may put them off.

In the next chapter we shall see that in interactions with babies, their gazing into your eyes and their smiles play a significant part in your communications.

Frowning

When someone draws his or her brows together in a frown, it can show that he or she is puzzled, anxious or displeased. It can be easy to conclude, at first glance, that someone is displeased, who is in fact frowning because of anxiety. So take all the circumstances into account, before jumping to conclusions about frowns. Is a father resentful about what you have said about his child – or could it be that you have raised anxieties for him?

OBSERVATION

- ☐ Watch a television play or soap opera for quarter of an hour but turn the sound off.
- ☐ Concentrate on how the actors use their faces.
- ☐ How easy is it to follow the story without words?
- ☐ Do different characters seem to have a different range of expressions?
- ☐ Which facial expressions give the clearest messages?

Bodies communicate

Many messages are conveyed by the way we use our bodies. We touch, turn away, or face someone, stand close or move apart, and make body movements and gesticulations. All of these are components of what is known as *body language*.

Touch

The most direct messages are those conveyed by touch, which can be playful, gentle, firm, careless or harsh. The extent to which people use touch varies between cultures. In Britain, for example, communicating through touch, except for a conventional handshake, is usually reserved for people who have a close relationship. Nevertheless, in certain work, such as hairdressing or medicine, staff are 'allowed' to touch people with whom they have no close personal relationship, but for professional reasons only. There are also occasions where touch cannot be avoided. This happens during the rush hour on crowded transport, when strangers do not treat contact with others as a form of personal communication.

Even within a society where using touch is not common, different people have their own style. Some happily put an arm round a friend's shoulder, or give delighted hugs to communicate their pleasure. Other, less demonstrative, people rely more on words or smiles to convey their feelings.

In your interactions with children, especially younger children, touch can be an important element of communication. It can convey unspoken messages such as 'I like you' or 'I am confident and you are safe in my hands'. For people caring for younger children, the sheer bodily care of children as you change, wash, dress and feed them, requires contact and closeness. It is also when children and staff get to know each other better. You can talk about what you are doing, take time to answer questions, sing songs and play games. Dressing a child can be just the time for playing finger games, or counting on their toes or playing knee-riding games like 'This is the way the ladies ride'.

Over and above the touching involved in physical care, touch and physical contact are necessary in playing and communicating with young children, especially with babies and toddlers. Stroking, hugging, cuddling, holding, bouncing and swinging can all convey important messages to the young children you work with: they tell them in a very direct way that you accept them and feel warm towards them.

Building warm respectful relationships, which is one of the main objectives of social pedagogy, does not always need words. Especially for younger children, touch is important. Unfortunately, touch can also pass on disrespectful messages, for example when staff handle children carelessly or are too hasty in how they deal with them. Then the message which children pick up on may be 'You are a nuisance and I wish this was over, so that I could do something really important.' The same is true for all people who are dependent on others for their physical care, such as disabled people or frail elderly people.

Reflection: things to discuss or think about

Consider this scenario: Janey is a nursey worker who likes her work, but there is a new toddler in her group who really seems to 'get under her skin'. He does not seem to co-operate when she dresses him and he hangs his head when she approaches. She is becoming more aware of this as the weeks go by. What should she do?

Unwanted touches

Since the late 1980s there has been a growing awareness of child sexual abuse and the need to protect children from this. Cases involving professional staff are rare, but have a high profile when they come to light. Service managers must be sensitive to children's vulnerability and take steps to reduce the risk of abuse. Procedures include carrying out police checks for any record of conviction, asking staff to declare any criminal record, scrutinising work histories for unexplained gaps, and taking up references. The ongoing support and supervision of staff and volunteers also provides an important safeguard. Ideally all children's services should have a clear policy about physical contact between adults and children and this should be communicated to, and discussed with, staff and volunteers.

All this is necessary, but it would be unfortunate if such precautions were to make staff self-conscious in their relationships with children and young people and uneasy about ever touching them. A touch, whether an arm round the shoulder or a hug, may be the most appropriate way of responding to a child who is in distress or who is enormously happy. Staff need to trust themselves and their own responses in these circumstances. In general, as children grow up, from babies and toddlers, through their early school years and into adolescence, casual friendly touching between children and adults outside the family decreases and becomes less appropriate; however there are also occasions when older children and teenagers show that they would welcome a hug. Workers who are sensitive to children and young people are, perhaps without realising it, sensitive to whether they would accept or reject physical contact. This should always be respected. Perhaps you can remember being reluctant to kiss a relative whom you hardly knew?

If children and young people are treated as people who have the right to be heard on any matter that concerns them, they also come to understand that they have the right to say 'no' to any unwanted touches, including being touched by others in their age group. It is also important that they feel free to tell a responsible adult about anything which causes them unease. For this to happen they must be consistently listened to and respected as partners in communication, rather than as merely subordinate to the adult members of staff. Listening attentively to other people is an important theme of this book which is treated in detail in later chapters.

It may be that a child or adolescent touches an adult worker in a way that the worker finds too intimate and unacceptable. If this happens the worker should make it clear that the behaviour is not appropriate. How this is done depends on the age of the child. A simple movement – removing a hand – might be enough; or the worker might need to give a clear verbal message that the behaviour is not acceptable (see pp.138–40 on boundaries). It would often be appropriate to mention such incidents to a senior worker.

More 'body language'

As well as through touch, there are three other important areas for communication through body language.

The orientation of the body

This means the extent to which you face someone or turn away during communication: whether you are alongside someone and looking in the same direction; or if you are facing them head on; whether you talk to them over your shoulder, or turn your back on them, not looking at them at all. Bodily orientation gives its own messages.

Imagine a foster carer putting out a snack for children coming home from school. A boy comes in, throws his school bag on the floor and gives a loud sigh. The carer speaks to the child over her shoulder, without turning to face him. This gives the message that she is not willing to give full attention to the child.

You can also receive information from other people's orientation towards yourself.

A child, who has been given a nursery place in an emergency, without any time for his parents to settle him in, turns away and hangs his head when you approach. You realise that he is still feeling strange and needs tactful attention.

Close or distant

The distance that people maintain between each another, and any changes in that distance can be significant messages about their feelings. In some societies adults usually stand or sit quite close. In others they 'keep their distance' unless they are near friends or relations. They can feel quite threatened if someone else comes too close. But when an adult and a child are communicating they often come very close, when they know one another.

Movements and gestures

Movements and gestures can convey meaning. These include such different gestures as waving a hand, shaking a fist, fidgeting with boredom or discomfort and tapping the foot in annoyance. Sometimes people performing these gestures are conscious of what they are doing. They may be waving goodbye or pointing something out. But people don't always realise that their movements give messages to other people. For example a colleague may smile when you say you are sorry for keeping her waiting and say 'It's quite all right,' but give away her true feeling by tapping her foot.

At this point a word of caution is necessary. It is not always easy to interpret non-verbal communication and you always need to take into account other aspects of what is happening, before jumping to conclusions about what any particular piece of 'body language' may mean. In the last example, if the colleague was tapping her foot in time to music on the radio, the movement would have quite a different meaning from a situation where she needed to speak to you about a young person experiencing difficulties.

OBSERVATION

☐ Spend quarter of an hour in a public place – station, park or shopping centre – and notice ways in which people use their bodies to communicate.

☐ Observe their facial expressions and watch their hands and feet.

☐ How close are people to each other?

☐ Do they touch?

☐ What is their physical orientation towards each other?

☐ What do you learn about the relationships between people from their body language? What feelings do they express?

Reflection: things to discuss or think about

• Why is knowing about interpersonal communication useful for staff who work with children and young people?

• In a summer playscheme, where the provider was very conscious of child abuse issues, staff were told that, for their own sakes, they must never touch a child unless they knew the reason for doing so, in advance – for example to comfort a child, to help them to use a swing, or to deal with an injury. This was so they might have an explanation in case a child or parent later made accusations against them. This approach is not followed by staff in another scheme. They often hug children, kiss them or take them on their knee, whether to comfort them, or as an expression of affection. They see their relationship with the children as a personal one, which includes a certain intimacy. What are the advantages and disadvantages of these two different approaches?

Interpersonal communication: key points

- Effective practitioners identify their professional aims and values and interact with other people in ways that help them to achieve their aims.

- For people working in a social pedagogic way, equality and respect for other people are important values.

- Interpersonal communication takes place when people – adults, teenagers, children and babies – are together and messages are sent backwards and forwards between them.

- These messages can be about ideas, feelings, facts or a mixture of these.

- The two main forms of interpersonal communication are verbal and non-verbal.

- Verbal communication is based on spoken words.

- Non-verbal communication consists of messages from one person to another conveyed by means other than words (although they can accompany words).

- Non-verbal communication includes the way people use their voices, facial expressions and bodies to convey meaning.

CHAPTER 2

Preverbal Communication

Although most of *Communication Skills for Working with Children and Young People* is for staff working with children and young people across the age range, this chapter is especially for people who work with babies. Babies also take part in communication. They cannot of course use words or, to begin with, understand them. Nevertheless, they have other ways of interacting with people. In social pedagogy all people are seen as being of value, whether very old or very young – in fact, whatever their age. Also everyone, including very young children, is seen as a member of society and a person in relationship with other people. For social pedagogues building and being drawn into relationships, on the basis of professional aims and values, is central to the work.

From the beginning, babies seem to be designed to communicate with those who care for them – they are very sociable beings. This makes the task of people who work with babies all the easier. As you carry out routine feeding, changing, bathing and when you play with them, it is not difficult to find yourself responding to babies, as well as taking the initiative. Together with their parents you will be playing your part in accompanying them into the rich experiences of human communication. While babies are born with great potential for communication, they also learn to communicate through their interactions with you and with their other caregivers. An obvious example is that they learn words and the use of words because you and other people talk to them.

Foster carers, nursery workers and childminders can play an important part in babies' becoming more and more effective as communicators. Their potential for communication will increase alongside their growing experience and intellectual development, as the years go by.

Babies and preverbal communication

In Chapter 1, we talked a little about effective communication, from a professional standpoint. To be an effective communicator, a person needs to be in control of their communication and to intend to communicate – for professionals, this includes communicating in such a way that their professional aims are well served. However, young babies do not have intentions in the way we usually understand the word, they do not think things over or make plans about what they are going to do, or how they are going to do it.

Communication at this stage of life is known as *preverbal* because it takes place before a child can talk. Nevertheless from birth babies are already equipped for the experiences which pave the way for communication:

- Babies find the people who look after them fascinating. They are drawn to look at another person's face and its movements. It has just the sort of simple pattern and contrasts of light and dark that capture their attention. Eyes, because they sparkle and move, are particularly fascinating.
- They are held by the sound of the human voice, especially when it is used in the special way that people have for talking to babies (see pp.35–7).

But it is not just that babies are attracted by other human beings. They themselves play their part in drawing you into communication with them, getting your attention and causing you to linger, play and talk. Babies soon learn that their actions bring about results – and particularly that they have an effect on other people. In the early months other people can be their most irresistible plaything.

Throughout the animal kingdom the characteristics and behaviour of young animals have a predictable effect on adult members of a species, which help the species to survive. Think how a mother bird is impelled to pop food into the open beak of a nestling. For human beings there seem to be similar processes at work.

Appearance

For many people a baby's appearance – the large eyes and forehead, tiny nose and, later, toddling walk – brings about a feeling of tenderness and protection. It is one of the signals which result in babies being looked after and responded to, that draw adults into communication with them.

Crying

For newborn babies a significant lesson is that when they cry someone turns up with comfort, food or attention. They are beginning to get some control over their environment. Babies who are always left to cry miss an important piece of learning.

Looking into your eyes

Your face, and especially your eyes, are fascinating for young babies. They hold your gaze with their own in a way that can be irresistible and leads you on to talk and play with them. When they have had enough, or want a few seconds rest, you will notice that they turn their eyes away, before seeking more interaction. Adults who are sensitive to the baby's signals do not try to prolong games or conversations longer than the baby wishes.

Smiling

By about two or three months of age, babies find a new and delightful way of attracting attention and engaging you in interaction - their first real sociable smiles when they look into your eyes. (You may notice even earlier smiles, but these are often in response to sensations in the digestive system, 'windy smiles'.) Adults find babies' smiles very rewarding and often work quite hard to get the baby to produce one.

Laughing

Some weeks after the first smile comes laughter. A baby's laugh can immediately draw you into play. Other signs of pleasure are the wriggles and squeals of delight when you approach and the special moment when a baby first holds out both arms to be lifted up.

Sounds

To start with the baby makes sounds that are rather haphazard and not very distinctive. Then at about four or five months, they start to make a cooing 'agoo' and like you to join in, saying the sound back, taking a turn in the conversation. This is a sound that you can get babies of just this age to repeat after you, once they can produce it spontaneously themselves. They also develop a more boisterous selection of sounds: spluttering, blowing raspberries, producing quite ear-splitting noises inviting you to join in the fun.

Look out for how they use lips and tongue in small movements, pushing the tongue out between the teeth, bringing the lips together and then breathing out with a little bubble of saliva. These early movements, co-ordinating breath with the articulation of tongue and lips, are part of the baby's early attempts at talking.

Towards seven months, babies produce sounds which are more like those found in adult speech. They produce consonants using the lips – like 'b' – and using the tongue – like 'd'. Also syllables such as 'ba' and 'da' make an appearance – all steps along the road to speech, which will develop very rapidly in the next year.

Babble and 'talk'

The syllables develop into repetitions: ba-ba, da-da-da-da-da; endless babbles, for the pleasure of hearing the sounds and the sensations they produce in the baby's mouth. Infants in most cultures, whatever language is spoken around them, make similar sounds at this stage and make them in the same sequence. However, by the time they have gone through this basic sequence, certainly by one year old, babies are moving towards whichever language they are accustomed to hearing. They now produce the sounds and intonation patterns of the language spoken by the people around them. They spend a lot of time pretending to talk, having conversations with themselves and with anyone else who wants to join in.

These are pretend conversations in which you can play your part, absorbed in the baby's contribution, imitating, pretending to understand, answering either in your own adult language or with sounds similar to baby's own. It may sound like fun – and it is – but it is also a way of leading the baby further into the world of communication.

Rituals and remembering

Before they reach their first birthday babies enjoy the games and rituals you build up together and recognise them as they fit into the nursery day. They remember the various signs that things are going to happen: the rattle of pans at dinner time, the jackets and scarves which mean it's time to go out. They are sensitive to your facial expression and can see when you are pleased and when you are cross. Words are also starting to carry meaning. At about eight months they understand 'No' and (may!) respond accordingly. Also, around this age some babies recognise their names and look round when called.

Letting you know how they feel

Towards the end of the first year crying and smiling are still powerful signals, but babies now have other ways of attracting your attention and letting you know what they want. They reach out for things beyond their grasp, pull at your clothing to get you to notice, and shake their heads vigorously or scuttle off in the opposite direction if they do not want to co-operate.

Games and imitation

By about ten months babies imitate your actions and those of other adults who hold an important place in their lives. They play peep-bo, clap hands and co-operate in games of pat-a-cake; they remember and use social gestures such as waving 'Bye-bye' and blowing kisses.

Babies learn about themselves

The sections above show some of the ways babies respond to you and get you to communicate. But as well as supplying their own part they are continually learning from you. By the time the baby is one year old, interacting with you and with other adults has played a major part in their developing potential as a communicator.

Over and above this, they are also learning about how you feel towards them, and how you value them as a human being. We shall see throughout this book that social pedagogues communicate respectfully with other people: they are open to the messages that come from other people and they respond sensitively towards them. Sensitive caregiving builds 'attachment' between the adults and children concerned. It provides children with emotional security, a feeling of worth, and is a protection against stress (for a discussion see Petrie *et al.* 2006, pp.11–13). The opposite is, unfortunately, also true.

OBSERVATION

☐ Spend some time observing a baby interacting with an adult. You might visit a local child welfare clinic, a mothers' or childminders' drop in centre, a nursery – or arrange to observe a parent and baby at home.

☐ Describe the part played by the baby in each episode of interaction – which may be short or prolonged.

☐ Include the following:

    O Does the baby seem to involve the adult in any interactions?

    O How does this happen – what does the baby do?

    O How does the baby respond to the adult?

    O Who seems to finish each interaction, the adult or the baby?

Adults and preverbal communication

If you watch someone who enjoys working with babies you'll notice that they behave as though the baby is a fully communicating person and already understands every word that is said. They treat babies as partners in communication whom they encourage to take their turn in 'conversations' and play; they listen to what the baby has to say; they ask plenty of questions such as: 'You like it don't you?' and: 'It's nice and warm, isn't it?', speaking in a special tone of voice, used just for babies, repeating themselves for the baby's benefit: 'Yes it's nice and warm.' They speak quite slowly and distinctly, sometimes with exaggerated changes of pitch and emphasis. They wait for the baby's reply, and if it is not forthcoming they supply it themselves. 'Mmm, I like that. That's nice.' This special way of talking to babies has been called 'motherese', because it seems to come naturally to many mothers. Meanwhile the baby gazes into the adult's face, watching and listening attentively, and taking their turn with movements, smiles and sounds.

Sensitive adults are attentive to all the information they receive from the baby. They time their actions, movements and words to synchronise, and fit in, with the actions of the baby. For example during feeds they allow themselves to be paced by the baby: they wait to speak, or to gently rock the baby, during the short intervals when the baby is not actually sucking. They go quiet when the baby starts to feed again. In fact they let the baby set the pace, gently responding to the noises he or she makes as though they were words.

Turn-taking

In this way, from the earliest days, babies are introduced to an important aspect of interpersonal communication – that we take turns, each listening while the other speaks and in episodes of play, waiting while the other person has a turn. Mothers and other caregivers constantly use questions as a way of showing that babies can take their turn in a 'conversation'. 'You like that, don't you?' the mother says to her two-month-old baby, long before there is any chance of the baby responding. Later in the book we shall return to turn-taking in adult conversations (see p.95).

OBSERVATION

☐ Observe an adult and baby and this time pay special attention to the part played by the adult.

☐ How does the adult talk to the baby?

☐ Do you notice any 'turn-taking'?

Labelling

Mothers often comment on their baby's experience, as it happens. For example the mother notices that the baby's attention is attracted to a bird outside the window and says 'It's a birdy, isn't it, yes, a bird having a drink of water.' Or she sees that the baby's attention is attracted to a noise outside and says 'What's that? What can you hear? It's a car, isn't it? Daddy's car.' The person close to the baby shares their experience and names it or labels it for them. 'You like that, don't you? Mmm, that's good,' says the foster carer, as the baby guzzles happily, or 'You're trying to get hold of my hair, aren't you?' as she avoids the baby's grasp.

Labelling means being attentive to the things the baby shows interest in and 'reflecting' (see Chapter 5) it back to them. It is different from pointing out and naming something that is interesting you. Indeed it is often difficult to get babies to pay attention to something 'out there' which they haven't noticed for themselves; for example they may not follow the direction of your finger if you point towards something.

You pick up what the baby notices

Because of labelling, repeated on many occasions, babies learn that there are words used to match their experience, for example the experience of seeing a dog is often accompanied by their carer saying 'dog'. This is one of the means by which children acquire language. When you label what a child is seeing, or experiencing through other senses, then you are seeing things from the child's point of view, you are entering their world. This is brought out in the training of social pedagogues and is an essential skill for people who work with young children and vital for sensitive communication.

Being sensitive to the baby's 'state'

People who are good at communicating are able to judge from various signals how the other person is feeling and to take this into account when they are communicating with them. As a nursery worker it is important when you're communicating with babies to be sensitive to their state of consciousness. This means how ready the baby is for communication and activity at any particular time. A baby's day has its own rhythm; at different times during the day the child goes from one state of consciousness to another. They pass from being deeply asleep, when it seems that nothing could disturb them, to a state of light sleep, when they are fidgeting and easily disturbed. They can pass from this to a state of wakefulness – fully alert and observant, but quite still. They may then enter a phase of activity and movement. This in turn can be followed by fussing and then by full-blown crying. They may then return to one of the previous states, including drowsiness and sleep.

A newborn baby spends most of the time asleep. Nevertheless there are many points during the day – often just after a feed – when a young baby is quiet, alert and ready for 'communication'. It is important to take advantage of these times and not just to put the baby straight back to sleep. These are the best times for conversation and play, if only for a few minutes.

As the baby grows, such times become more frequent and longer. When babies are restless it could be that they are tired and will soon sleep. But you may find that you can bring them to a state of quiet attention – the state in which they are most able to take in what is happening – by talking, stroking, rocking them or showing them something interesting.

When they are crying, on the other hand, there is so much interference (see p.47) from noise, movement and discomfort that they are not able to attend to anything else. At these times it is better to soothe a baby rather than to attempt more playful communications.

OBSERVATION

☐ Observe a baby, whether with an adult or alone, for 20 minutes. Describe the 'state' that he or she is in and any changes in it during the observation period.

☐ Notice the following:

  O How much movement is there? Observe the baby's arms, legs, trunk, head.

  O What sounds does the baby make?

  O Are they interested in what is happening around them?

  O How absorbed is the baby in any activity – for example a feed, a game or conversation?

  O If the baby is asleep how would you describe the sleep? Is it light, restless or deep? What is the baby doing that leads you to this judgement?

  O Is anything responsible for bringing about a change from one state to another, during the course of the observation?

Reflection: things to discuss or think about

'You have to be really skilled to work well with babies.'

'Looking after babies comes naturally.'

'Babies are not as interesting as older children.'

- What do you think of these different points of view?
- What answers would you give, making use of what you have read in this chapter?
- Why would social pedagogues want to respond to babies sensitively?

Preverbal communication: key points

- Preverbal communication is communication in which one of the people involved has not yet developed language: for example communication between an adult and a baby.

- Social pedagogues believe that all people, whatever their age, are valuable and that they convey this understanding in how they communicate and relate to other people, including babies.

- Babies have great potential as communicators and can, if you let them, draw you into 'conversation' and play.

- Communicating with babies includes talking to them, touching them and playing with them. Sensitive and responsive communication is very important for a baby's well-being and development, emotionally and intellectually.

- People who enjoy looking after babies talk to them as though they understand. They use a special style of talking which attracts and holds the child's attention; they time their contributions so that they fit in with those of the baby; they 'take turns' with the baby.

- Babies are most ready for talk and play when they are wakeful and alert. In this state they are better able to take things in than when they are fussing or sleepy.

CHAPTER 3

Careful Listening

The next three chapters are about listening – a core skill for people who work with children and young people. In social pedagogy, the worker is aware of people as whole people, listening, observing and responding to their spoken and unspoken communications.

Interpersonal communication is a two-way process, whatever the age of the people involved. It is sometimes helpful to think of one person sending a message and someone else receiving it. If no messages pass backwards and forwards then communication does not take place. So, while talking has a part to play, listening (and observing) are also essential. In other words it is vital for you to be able to listen carefully so as to take in the information other people give you. Think of the occasions when you need to listen, and to listen carefully.

- Throughout the day children have much to tell you about. They confide problems, explain games, ask for help, pass on jokes.

- Parents tell you important details about their children – about sleep patterns, their likes and dislikes at meal times, information about the child's health.

- People pass on changes in family and household arrangements that may affect a young person.

- Parents may want to talk about personal problems.

- Colleagues pass on new working arrangements because another member of staff is absent.

- Other professional workers may ask you to follow a certain course of action, for example a speech therapist may want you to help a child who has problems being understood; or a social worker explains the arrangements for a teenager to have contact with their parents.

All these people need to be listened to carefully for the following reasons:

- Careful listening means that you co-operate better with other people because you understand 'messages' that are important for your work.

- Listening to what people say is an excellent way of coming to understand them, of developing your relationship and encouraging them to communicate with you. It also presents them with a model of how to treat other people. The social pedagogue should always be aware that they are role models for many of the people they are working with.

- When you listen carefully to someone they realise that you are taking them and their experience seriously, that you treat what they have to say with respect.

There is a new awareness of the child's right to be heard on matters that concern them. It can be found in much legislation including the Children Act (1989) and the *United Nations Convention on the Rights of the Child* (1989). Children should have the experience of being listened to from the beginning; it builds their self-esteem and sense of being a person. As we remarked in the last chapter, children and young people need staff who are responsive and sensitive to them and relationships which they can trust. As you listen attentively to what they say, you come to know them better and begin to see things from their point of view. Social pedagogy stresses the importance of being able to take on other people's perspectives, being able to put yourself in their shoes and trying to see the world as they see it. This is based on an understanding that each person has his or her own 'life world': they have their own history and experience, they are affected in particular ways by society and they have developed their own way of making sense of their place in the world.

Exercise: accurate listening

- Find a partner and take turns to listen carefully to one another.

- You each have five minutes, more or less, to tell the other how you came to choose your present job, about any previous experience you have had, and any preferences about the sort of work you do.

- After one person has spoken the other – the listener – repeats what he or she can remember, with as much detail as possible.

- The speaker does not interrupt, but when the listener has finished says if anything has been left out, or is inaccurate.

- When you have each had a turn as speaker and as listener, share with one another how you found the exercise – for example if you found it hard to listen carefully, or if you thought it was hard to talk.

Listening can be difficult!

While listening is very important it is not always easy.

Here are two imaginary situations. The first is something of a dream world and the second a nightmare.

Dream nursery

Here everyone listens carefully. The nursery worker just says 'Will people please listen for a moment?' and all the children stop playing and look towards her, even Amira – who has just managed to get hold of the doctor's stethoscope which she has wanted all morning – becomes attentive; Wayne stops crying about his cut knee; the budgie in her cage stops chirping and swinging on her bell. Everyone is listening.

When parents come in the workers listen carefully to what they have to say; Cheryl, listening to a child's father, doesn't seem to notice two children pulling at her clothes for attention, nor that the twins are attacking one another with paint.

The parents also listen carefully to the nursery staff, even when they are in a hurry and are worried about getting to work on time.

And the staff are noted for the way they stop what they are doing – changing nappies, explaining what causes rain to a three-year-old – in order to pay attention to another worker.

Nightmare playscheme

This is a fairly typical day at nightmare playscheme. No one ever really listens to anyone else. A mother, who looks rather worried, is explaining to a playworker that her little boy has not slept well and is a bit off his food. She wondered whether to bring him today, but she felt she could not afford to miss work. All the time she is talking, the playworker is gazing out of the window, wondering if she can get out during her lunch hour to buy food for her evening meal.

The children do not listen to anyone; they all seem to live in worlds of their own. They cannot get anyone else to play or co-operate, because no one pays attention.

The parents are too anxious to listen to the staff properly. They think that the staff are often critical and so they are always on the defensive and do not take in necessary information that staff give them. When it is the day for swimming, few children are sent with costumes, even though staff often remind parents in person.

As for staff meetings these are angry occasions where people talk but do not listen. There are lots of interruptions and voices are often raised. Strangely enough the louder the voices the less they are heard!

Shouting does not help people to listen

Reflection: things to discuss or think about

- Both of these impossible establishments are fictitious but they both point to one conclusion: listening is not always easy. What reasons can you find for this in the accounts of the two establishments given above?

- You can probably think of your own examples of circumstances which make listening difficult, whether at work or in everyday life.

Listening and hearing are not the same

It is important to understand that listening and hearing are not the same. While I am writing I am hardly aware of the sounds around me but, when I stop and listen, I can hear a car outside in the street, somewhere a radio is playing and there are voices outside my door.

These sounds were there all the time but they were not claiming my attention. I was preoccupied with what I was writing and so was not getting strong messages from outside. It was almost as though I had taken a telephone off the hook and no calls were coming through.

Something similar can happen in conversation. In certain circumstances, although I can hear the other person perfectly well what they are saying does not get through. It is as though the information they wish to pass on is sabotaged in some way. Either it is completely blocked, or something does not register or, in some cases, whatever gets through is distorted and muddled. Let me give you some examples of what I mean, when listening is difficult:

1. A residential care worker is getting out brightly coloured papers, paint and glue so that young people can make masks. He is quite excited about it because he went to a mask-making training course, last week, and can see endless possibilities. Suddenly he realises that he can't find a bag of tinsel, left over from last year's Christmas tree. He rummages about in the bottom of his bag, but can't find it. A boy comes in and says that he's had a rotten day at school. 'Did you?' the worker asks, automatically, 'poor thing,' at the same time turning out the contents of the bag on to the floor and rapidly sorting

through. He has not registered that the boy is really quite upset, because he is too preoccupied with finding the tinsel. The boy sees he is not interested and wanders off.

2. A childminder is asking a mother if she could bring in a new supply of disposable nappies. The mother, meanwhile, is watching engrossed as her baby reaches out for a rattle and, for the first time in her life, manages to successfully grasp hold of it. The next day, she does not bring the nappies. Although in one sense she 'heard' the minder's voice (sound waves caused her eardrum to vibrate and nerves carried impulses to her brain) the mother was not listening; the minder's words made no impression on her.

3. A playworker is telling a mother, over the phone, that her child has had a seizure. The mother immediately feels anxious. The worker says that the child seems to be fine now and that the staff have given the child the medication which the mother had left in case this should happen. He explains the details of what happened and the severity and length of the fit. When she puts the phone down the mother finds it difficult to remember in any detail what he has told her.

4. A mother is about to take her turn on a family centre's voluntary rota, for the first time. Her child has only attended for a few days. She is quite nervous, and worries in case her child is 'naughty' or over-demanding. The worker talks to her and says that the best thing for her to do is to give as much attention to her own child as he seems to need and not to bother about anything else. 'He'll soon find his feet,' she says. But the mother does not seem to take in what the worker says. It does not fit her image of being a helper and she continues to feel guilty that she needs to give so much attention to her own child. As a result neither she nor the child is happy.

5. An inexperienced student teacher looks at a child's drawing of two people. 'My nan has gone to the hospital with my grandpa,' he says. The teacher is very concerned that the children should start to learn elementary mathematical ideas.

'Oh, yes,' she answers, looking at the picture, 'Which is the bigger one? Which is the smaller one?' She does not seem to have listened to what could have been an important message from the child.

Interference

It is just as necessary to listen carefully to children as it is to listen carefully to adults. High-quality listening shows that you respect people, that you think their experience, the things they tell you about and the questions they ask, are important to you. It is also a way of encouraging them to communicate with you – no one likes to be ignored or constantly misunderstood. But as we have seen people, whether they are children or adults, are not always successful in their communications. The messages don't get through for many reasons – somewhere there is *interference* which blocks the way, either completely or only letting some parts of a message through. Interference can come from the speaker (the person who is sending the information) or the listener (the receiver). Sometimes there may be interference from both together! When this happens there is little chance of communication.

Below are some sources of interference, reasons why people cannot receive the verbal messages that are sent to them.

Reasons for interference and how to help
Hearing
When someone has some hearing loss, then obviously they find listening difficult and you have to be especially careful when you talk to them. The person with hearing impairment needs to see your face and lip movements easily, and you should make an effort to speak more distinctly. For a deaf adult, you should write down any important information. There may be a teacher for the deaf, or another special needs worker, who can give you advice about this.

Some services may train workers to use British Sign Language to use with hearing-impaired children and young people. Just as deaf children learn to lip read spoken language, hearing children can soon become familiar with some words in BSL.

Speech

There may be some speech defect or impairment, for example if someone has a stutter you will have to be especially patient in order to understand and to respond. Over time, this will give them assurance that you are there for them, that you accept them and believe that they are valuable. Sometimes additional professional help is needed. For example, if a speech therapist is working with a child and their family it is good for staff to understand the approach that is being taken so that they can co-operate.

Not having the same language

If you understand a few words of another person's language, and they understand a little of yours, much can still be done just by trying to communicate – persevering patiently and carefully, using plenty of gestures until you make sense to one another – and a challenge like this can be fun. On other occasions, where understanding is vital, it is necessary to use an interpreter. It is good to keep a list of local people who can be called on to interpret when necessary and to translate written communications.

Children still acquiring language

A young child's language is still immature so they may not understand adult speech properly and may also have difficulties in being understood. As you come to know a child you soon get on to the same wavelength, find ways of saying things so that they understand and learn to figure out what they are trying to communicate. Again this needs patience but it is an essential part of your work and you should spend as much time as you can getting to know children who are new to a service, helping them to get used to you. Children need people who are sensitive and responsive towards them if they are to get on well and be happy. And you can't be sensitive towards a child until you can understand their 'messages', what their words, their gestures and their expressions mean; these are some of the building blocks of your relationship.

Even older children can have difficulty in understanding you, and you them. If you have not shared much experience together either of you may refer to events or use expressions which leave the other perplexed. If you see that a child is struggling to understand, to make sense of what you are saying, you have to make extra efforts and find new ways of explaining.

Distractions

Distractions are all the claims on your attention that can stop you from listening. Here are some possibilities:

- discomfort, for example when a stuffy room is used for a staff meeting
- physical pain, such as a headache
- interruptions, as when a colleague wants to speak to you and a child is trying to get your attention at the same time
- emotions like anger, anxiety or sadness which block or distort incoming or outgoing messages
- thinking about other matters – a problem at home or at work, or day dreaming about some pleasant event
- noise, which makes concentration difficult.

Avoiding distractions

Distractions in yourself

As someone who works with people, you need to be aware of any potential distractions, whether for yourself or others. Once you are aware of them you can take steps to avoid potential distractions so that effective interpersonal communication may be possible. When social pedagogues reflect on their practice, they think about how they have reacted to what was going on, as well as to things they have observed. In the light of this self-knowledge they can then make decisions about how to react in future.

If you are aware of distractions within yourself, like a headache, or feelings of anxiety, or wanting to think about other things, then you need to remind yourself to listen as carefully as you can. Sometimes you may decide that this is not the right time or place to listen to someone properly. For example, you could tell a fellow member of staff that at the moment things are a bit hectic and ask if they could tell you some personal news later. At other times you may decide that it is very important to listen now and not to put someone off. For example a young person comes home to her foster carer, obviously upset. She asks if she can have a word with the foster carer. The foster carer explains to a different child, who wants her to come to look at the rabbits *now*, that she will do so later, but now she is going to listen to what the other young person has to say. Perhaps she chooses to listen to the young person in a quieter or more private room.

It's difficult to concentrate in certain situations

Distractions in other people

If, on the other hand, you sense that the other person is distracted in such ways, then you will need to take great care with your communication. It may be a good idea to ask if the other person has got some immediate concern that is preoccupying them. Or you may need to repeat what you have to say and check that it has been understood. This is especially helpful if you have to pass on details that the other person might find alarming. For example if you need to explain to a parent that their child has bumped his head and been taken to hospital for a check-up. Often the parent needs to ask for more explanation, repeating the same questions, and getting you to say more than once what has happened. In such cases it is helpful to ask 'Is there anything you would like me to go over about what happened?' and allow the parent enough time to check out what she still needs to know.

Children and young people, also, must not be distracted if they are to listen properly. You may be having an interesting, important conversation with young children when suddenly the window cleaner appears at the window. If the outside competition is too strong, it is pointless trying to go on with your previous conversation. In any case what is actually happening before the children's eyes is much more fascinating for them. It can be a starting point for children's play, for many activities and for further interesting conversations. If your earlier conversation was really important, then you will just have to find another time for it, when the children are not distracted.

You can see if someone else, of whatever age, is paying attention to what you are saying. A listening baby is quiet, their limbs are still and their eyes hold your gaze in a look of concentration and expectancy. When people of any age look at the person who is talking, when they do not interrupt or fidget, these are signs that they are probably listening. If these signs are absent, you will know that what you want to convey is having difficulty getting through.

What about 'clear speech'?

You may be surprised to have come so far in this book without reading that it is important to speak clearly in order to communicate well. This understanding is, however, too simple. Clear, careful speech is often necessary, but it is not always sufficient for getting your message across.

Someone who speaks clearly does not necessarily get their messages across to another person more effectively than someone who does not. People who speak distinctly, with perfect grammar, may still fail to communicate. Effective communication requires that a person must also take into account factors which are likely to be sources of interference and do what they can to avoid or eliminate them. Imagine talking about the meanings of 'high' and 'low' or 'round' and 'square' to a child who is upset and crying. However clear and simple the explanation and however careful and correct the speech, the child would understand little. Similarly, it might be better to choose another time to discuss exam options with a teenager who is waiting anxiously for a text message.

In neither case would it be sensible to protest 'But I explained very clearly.' Clear explanations are not always enough. People don't even need to speak at all clearly, or use good grammar, in order to be understood perfectly. This may be the case between close friends and relatives, people who are very familiar to one another. For them a few words and gestures 'Did you get the…' and 'I asked but…' may convey all the meaning necessary.

But people who have a less close relationship need to speak more clearly to one another, in order to be properly understood. In formal situations, like work – including work with children – people become more formal in their speech and take more care with what they say and how they say it. Staff should be more careful of their speech at work than would be necessary at home. And, as was suggested earlier, it is often especially important to take much more care in situations where there is likely to be interference (see p.47).

Reflection: things to discuss or think about

- What in your experience is the most common sort of interference to get in the way of communication?

- Do you think people listen as carefully to children and young people as they do to adults?

- Why is it important to listen to children and young people?

- What would you reply to someone who said 'They are too young to know what's best for them – so why should we bother listening to them?'

OBSERVATION

☐ Become aware of any sources of interference when you are listening or trying to listen.

☐ Does your attention wander when someone is talking to you? Make notes of any occasions when this happens as soon as possible after the event and say why you were finding listening difficult.

☐ Look out for instances when you think that someone is not really listening – perhaps to you. How do you know? Make notes about what happened.

Careful listening: key points

- In interpersonal communication listening and observing are as important as speaking.

- Careful listening is essential when you work with people: children, young people, parents and colleagues should be listened to carefully.

- By listening to someone you learn about their perspective on the world (their 'life world'). This is essential for building a relationship with them and is a key principle for social pedagogy.

- Careful listening shows respect and helps to avoid muddles. Listening to people helps you to get to know them and can encourage them to communicate with you.

- Careful listening is not always easy and 'interference' can occur. Interference means that a message is blocked or distorted. Sometimes the interference comes mainly from the person who sends the message and sometimes from the person receiving it.

- Sources of interference include: hearing and speech impairments, not understanding each other's language properly and distractions arising, for example, from discomfort, interruptions and strong emotions.

- Staff need to be alert to the possibility of interference when they are talking and listening to others and should do what they can to eliminate it. Effective communication takes place when messages get through clearly, without being blocked or distorted.

CHAPTER 4

Being an Encouraging Listener

If you spend any time observing someone who works with children you will see them taking part in a variety of interpersonal communication. You will see them giving and asking for advice and explanation, posing questions, making jokes, asking for help and listening. Chapter 3 showed how listening carefully is important for effective communication. In this chapter we turn to being an *encouraging listener*, the sort of listener who enables other people, adults and children, to communicate to the best of their ability. We have already seen that you need to be aware of and, if possible, avoid *interference*. Encouraging listening is to go one step further by giving other people your full attention and – this is essential – letting them know they have your full attention.

One of the professional aims of social pedagogues is that the people they are working with participate as fully as possible in all the matters that concern them – social participation. The opposite of social participation is when people are 'marginalised' – that is they are left on the edge, not really taking part and, especially relevant to this chapter, what they have to say is not listened to. This is where encouraging listening comes in. Let's look at some encouraging listening in action.

1. In an adventure playground, the playleader, Sally, is carrying out a safety inspection up on the platform of a play structure. Ian climbs up beside her, sobbing and saying that his brother has just attacked him. Sally sees that he is upset and decides that the first priority is to hear him out. She stops what she is doing and crouches down beside him. Sharing his level she

can give him much more attention than looking down on the top of his head. He can see and hear her better, as well. She gives him her complete concentration and listens to him without interrupting. As Ian realises that she is truly listening, he calms down, he expresses himself more clearly and his story becomes easier to understand.

2. It is the end of the afternoon when Renata's mother asks if this is a good time to ask Jenny, the early years worker, about something. As it happens this is a convenient moment and so Jenny takes her out into the garden where it's fairly quiet. At first the mother is hesitant; her story is complicated involving her former partner and problems that arise after Renata's fortnightly visits to see him. Renata seems disturbed and doesn't settle down to sleep easily; she is also having quite a few tantrums. Jenny listens quietly. She occasionally nods her head, smiles her assurance that she is listening and takes her part in the conversation by means of the odd word of encouragement, 'I see...', 'Yes...', 'Mmm...' She asks no questions and offers no advice or explanations. Renata's mother seems to find this enough, for the moment; she becomes less hesitant and starts to communicate more clearly. At this point attentive, encouraging listening is what she needs most from Sally.

This sort of listening may not be easy for people who are unfamiliar with it. You may find that you desperately want to interrupt with a question, give your point of view, or offer some advice. Questions and advice may become appropriate but when someone is upset they are not helpful in the first instance. They could change the subject away from what the other person is anxious to discuss, towards something which is much more what you want to talk about yourself. In fact anything except encouraging listening could have the effect of shutting up someone who needs to talk. Attentive, encouraging listening can help someone let what is worrying them come to the surface, while offering advice or asking too many questions could be frustrating.

For example, Michael is worried about his child, Sean; he thinks that Sean is not eating enough. At the back of his mind is the memory of his own younger brother who was always sickly and died when he was ten years old. Yesterday evening Sean ate practically nothing and he has had no breakfast today. Michael is beginning to feel that he cannot cope. He is a single parent and does not have very frequent contact with the rest of his family.

The teaching assistant hardly gives Michael a chance to explain what is on his mind but rushes straight in with reassurances that the child is perfectly healthy, that children eat what they need to eat and that there is no cause to worry. She tells him about other children who eat little but grow up strong and healthy. When Michael continues to express his worries the teaching assistant starts to ask questions. Is the child having too many snacks between meals, she wants to know?

Michael is put off by both the information and the questions but nevertheless answers to the best of his ability. He is not helped, however, and goes away still burdened with an anxiety he needed to share.

The next day he approaches another, more experienced, member of staff with his worry. This worker sees that Michael is very anxious, so she quietly hears him out before she gets round to making some suggestions. He is very relieved that she is obviously really listening and he feels able to confide the story of his brother. He feels that it is a relief to get this out in the open. When she feels that he has said what is in his mind the worker reassures him and offers some suggestions. He goes away feeling less anxious and able to take up the worker's advice.

Use 'encouraging listening' when it is appropriate

It is essential to become aware of the times when you really need to give your full attention and encouragement to others, adults and children, so that they find it easy to talk, rather than yourself taking a more equal part in the conversation. Putting other people's needs first is how effective social pedagogues set about achieving their professional aims. Encouraging listening is especially helpful when the other person is very excited or upset or has a great deal they need to say. It can also encourage someone who is shy to say what is on their mind.

When you first try to listen in this way, encouraging the other person to speak rather than making your own contribution, you may feel that it is rather artificial. On the other hand it may seem perfectly natural. The art is in using encouraging listening at the right time. Obviously if the other person is eager to hear your point of view, or asks straightforwardly for advice, it is very frustrating for them if you do not take your part in the conversation.

How to be an encouraging listener

Here are some ways to be a good, encouraging listener.

- Attend carefully to what the other person is saying – you may need to make a conscious effort to ignore distractions.
- Let them know that you are listening, using non-verbal communication. Remember to:
  - keep your body and your head turned towards them
  - with children, get down to their level if necessary
  - do not move away
  - use nods and smiles (where appropriate), to encourage them to continue talking
  - look at them while they are talking – do not let your gaze wander about as though you are thinking about other things.
- Let them know that you are listening, by using verbal communication:
  - use encouraging words and sounds like 'yes', 'I see', 'Mmm'.
  - Wait until they have finished what they have to say – interruptions are often frustrating and may discourage nervous people from speaking. *Don't butt in!*
  - Avoid questions (unless there is something you really do not understand), explanations or advice – at any rate for the time being.

On many occasions this sort of listening is more valuable than having a discussion about a problem. You show by your encouragement that you are interested, that the speaker is not boring you and that you are putting their needs first. It's just a case of giving someone space to talk over whatever is on their mind. This helps them to think things through and often they can come up with their own solutions.

Reflection: things to discuss or think about

- What is most difficult about being a good listener?
- Have you ever been in a position where you would really have liked someone to listen whole-heartedly to you? Is it easy to find people who are willing to listen?
- What sorts of situations come up at work (or practice placement) when people need listening to?

Exercise: encouraging listening

- Find another person with whom to practise encouraging listening.
- Each think about a situation that presents some problem that you are happy to share – perhaps about a child you work with or some other subject concerned with your job or training.
- Take turns to tell each other about the problem. Each has five minutes.
- Use 'encouraging' listening, as described on pp.57–8. At the end of each turn share with one another what the experience has been like. What was it like to be the listener and what was it like to be listened to attentively?

OBSERVATION

☐ Become aware of the quality of listening in your place of work, college, home or elsewhere.

☐ During the course of the next week be on the look-out for any time when someone listens carefully and attentively to another person and the effect this has. (The speaker can be either adult or child; so can the listener.) Does this happen frequently?

☐ Look out for interruptions when someone is speaking. What happens? How does the speaker react?

☐ Practise encouraging listening if an opportunity comes up where you feel it would be helpful. Make notes about what happened, why you thought encouraging listening should be used and how the speaker reacted.

Encouraging listening: key points

- A professional principle of social pedagogues is that the people with whom they are working participate as fully as possible in the matters that concern them. Using encouraging listening can be a first step towards this, because it builds confidence in the other person.

- Sometimes people, whatever their age, just need to be listened to. They don't need questions, advice or opinions. These can come later if necessary.

- Just being listened to can encourage a person to communicate what is on their mind and can sometimes help them to sort out problems for themselves. It can also help them to calm down if they are feeling flustered.

- The main ways to be an encouraging listener are: not to interrupt, to keep the flow of speech going by using encouraging words, sounds and nods, to look at the person while they are talking and not to make your contribution until they have finished what they wish to say.

CHAPTER 5

Feedback

Skilled communicators are aware of the various factors in play in interpersonal communication, and reflect on their work accordingly. In this chapter we will discuss the concept of 'feedback' and how this relates to interpersonal communication.

The psychologists who developed ways of thinking about interpersonal communication and the social skills involved based some of their ideas on practical skills like using tools or driving a car (Hargie 2010). An important concept for understanding practical skills is feedback. Feedback comes about as a direct result of your actions. The term covers the processes involved in performing a task and being 'fed' information about how you are doing so that you adjust your performance, accordingly.

For example, if you are cutting a channel in a piece of wood you may feel that the wood is softer than at first you thought, and also see that the chisel is cutting too deeply. These are two pieces of feedback about your action and because of them, almost automatically, you lighten the pressure of your hand on the chisel. To take another example, while driving, you look at the speedometer and notice that you are going faster than you had thought. This information is feedback about how you are driving and, as a result, you take your foot off the accelerator, the car goes slower and the speedometer shows your new lower speed.

Feedback in interpersonal communication

The idea of feedback is also used in thinking about interpersonal communication. Here feedback is used for all the verbal and non-verbal 'messages' that pass between people in the course of an interaction.

All of these have an effect on how two individuals communicate and what they communicate to each other.

In interpersonal communication feedback can be either *positive* or *negative*. When you listen in an encouraging way (see Chapter 4) you are giving the other person positive feedback in the form of encouraging sounds, nods, smiles and words. They are aware of these 'messages' which assure them that you are interested in what they say and that it is all right to go on talking. In this way you assist the person to communicate confidently and you build their trust in you and in themselves – one of the aims of social pedagogy. If you were to frown, or turn away, the other person would feel you were not interested in them or even that you were hostile towards them. You would be giving them negative feedback which would have its own negative results. They might, for example, stop talking altogether, or they might become aggressive in order to get their message through.

Here are some more examples of feedback:

1. A residential care worker can see that a young person does not understand what she is telling him because he looks puzzled. She finds a different way of explaining to him, using simpler words.

2. A nursery nurse tells a father about a forthcoming visit from the nursery doctor when his child can have a routine developmental check. As she speaks she sees, from his expression, that the father is unnecessarily alarmed. So she reassures him that this is just a routine developmental check-up, available for all the nursery children. The father visibly relaxes.

3. A foster carer is worried about one of the children she's looking after, who seems to be getting very little sleep. She speaks to the child's social worker about it, but thinks that the social worker, who is smiling, is not taking her concern seriously – so she raises her voice. The social worker stops smiling and apologises. The carer starts to speak in a more normal tone of voice.

4. A playworker wants to tell a colleague about an idea she has for publicising a fund-raising event. As she starts, hesitantly

at first, she can see from her colleague's reaction that he is interested in what she has to say. The colleague does not interrupt, looks towards her and smiles in agreement. She is encouraged to develop her idea and tell him all about it.

Such feedback passes backwards and forwards during all interpersonal communication letting both parties know how their messages are being received. Sometimes people are aware of the feedback they are giving to other people, but sometimes they are less conscious of how they are coming across. For example with straightforward verbal feedback like 'What a good idea' or 'I don't understand' the speaker is conscious of the message they are sending. With non-verbal feedback – such as frowns, smiles, or fidgeting, they may be less aware of the 'messages' they are sending out.

Communicating by telephone

Perhaps the main reason people sometimes find it difficult to leave a message on an answerphone is that there is no feedback whatsoever. After the beep you are on your own, and it can feel like talking into thin air! We all expect – and need – feedback in everyday communication. But an answerphone cannot support our communication in the way we are used to simply because it is not a person: talking to an answerphone is not interpersonal communication! Even an ordinary telephone conversation can sometimes be a problem, especially when it is about a difficult subject. This is because the feedback received is so limited compared with what we are accustomed to in face-to-face conversations.

Imagine a childminder using the phone to ask a mother if she is going to bring her child in today – it is after the time the child usually arrives and the childminder wants to go out shopping. She will wait if the child is going to come in, but otherwise she would like to get out before the shops are crowded. Over the phone she gets no feedback from the mother's body language or facial expressions. She cannot see the mother's look of dismay, and the despondent shrug of her shoulders so she does not adjust what she says accordingly. If she had been able to observe these signs, she might have asked if there was any problem.

But even on the phone there is some feedback, over and above the verbal communication, the actual words which are used. People use their voices in various ways, intentionally and otherwise. They pause, hesitate, speak quickly or slowly, they are quiet or loud, sigh, click their tongues, laugh, yawn, let their voices rise to a higher pitch or fall lower. All of these non-verbal communications are feedback that can be picked up on the phone and which can affect the way a sensitive listener responds.

Using the phone

- Phone calls deprive those at each end of the phone of feedback. It is wiser, therefore, not to use the phone to communicate sensitive material – difficult problems about a child, for example – unless it is absolutely necessary.

- You need to listen even more carefully on the phone than in everyday conversations. Especially be alert to *how* people are speaking as well as to the words used.

- Remember that the other person cannot see you, either, and they have no clues from your body language as to what you mean. You need to express what you have to say really clearly.

- It is useful to be really sure of what you have to say before you make a call. Start by greeting the other person, say who you are and the main thing you are phoning about, for example, 'Hello, this is June Grey from Hillside Play Centre. I'm ringing about paying for the minibus we hired last week.'

Exercise: telephone communication

Sit back to back with a partner, so that you can't see each other, and role play some of the following phone calls. Take turns to play each part.

1. A member of staff in a residential home rings the suppliers to ask why washing-up liquid and other cleaning materials have not been delivered. They were ordered a month ago. Staff are constantly having to go out to buy cleaning things.

The person at the other end cannot recall receiving the order. She needs to know when it was sent and other details.

2. A mother rings a playgroup to tell them that her son does not want to come in because something has upset him at the playgroup. She does not know what it is, but he is really upset. She wants to know if anything untoward has happened that staff are aware of and asks what she should do.

   At the other end of the line, the playworker is puzzled. She cannot think of anything. She would like to talk to the mother face to face and thinks that she should see the child and talk to him, also.

Reflection: things to discuss or think about

- Do you think that you are more aware or less aware of feedback in interactions with babies and children, than of feedback in interactions with adults?

- Are there any differences in the sort of feedback received from babies, children and adults? What are they?

- Why is it important to be alert to feedback in personal work?

OBSERVATION

☐ Be on the look-out for feedback given to children about their communications and any feedback they give to other people.

☐ Spend 15 minutes watching a television play or soap opera, concentrating on one character and the feedback they give to others about their communications. Do they welcome communication? Block it? Understand it? How do they give feedback, verbally or non-verbally?

Reflecting back

Reflecting back is a special form of feedback which is useful to have at your command when you need to let someone know that you have heard and understood them.

Reflecting back is when you repeat to the speaker the main thing which he or she has just said; it is as though you are a mirror for them. Although this sounds as though the other person might find what you say boring, or obvious, in the right circumstances people welcome reflecting back as a demonstration that you have really heard and understood them.

With practice it becomes easy to reflect back without sounding wooden. There is no need to repeat everything that is said, just the main points, in your own words. Here are some examples.

Example 1

> FATHER (*unavoidably late and rather agitated*): I've been trying to get you all day to say I'd be late but I couldn't get through, the phone was always engaged.
>
> WORKER (*reassuringly*): You tried again and again but we were always engaged.

Reflecting back is useful in this case because the worker lets the father know that she appreciates that he has tried to co-operate. This is not the only sort of feedback a worker could give in this situation. How the worker responds depends on her judgement about the best outcome in this incident. For example, if the father was continually late, the worker might have chosen to discuss this with him (we shall look at confrontation in Chapter 11). Or, if the father had a lot to say about the reasons for his lateness (say his wife had been in a car accident) the worker might have chosen to listen to him attentively and encouragingly without reflecting back. Sometimes a speaker just wants to be listened to.

Example 2

> TEENAGER (*new to her foster carer, showing a photo*): This is my mum, and this is my dad and this is my baby and this is me in my house.
>
> FOSTER CARER: That's a picture of you at home and your family.

Reflecting back is reassuring for someone who is shy. In this case it tells the child that they have been heard and focuses the conversation on what is important to him or her at this moment. It will encourage them to say more if they wish to and the foster carer could make further responses. On the other hand, if the foster carer were to change the subject to something she thought would be 'less upsetting' for the new arrival, it could leave the teenager feeling rejected. This would not be a good basis for building a trusting relationship between them.

Example 3

> FIRST RESIDENTIAL CARE WORKER: He's already had his medicine this morning, but could you remind him to take a spoonful after his other meals?
>
> SECOND WORKER: OK – he should have one spoonful after lunch and another after tea?

This worker is using reflecting back to check that she has understood the instructions she has been given. It gives the first worker a chance to correct any misunderstandings.

Exercise: reflecting back

- Find a partner and take it in turns to talk about:
  - last weekend: what you most enjoyed, what you least enjoyed and why, or
  - your placement (or work): what you most enjoy, what you least enjoy and why.

- Allow each other five minutes to talk. The task of the listener is to reflect back – the speaker should make the task easy by stopping frequently to give the listener chance to reflect back.

- This may feel artificial (it is!) but it gives you an opportunity to experience and practise reflecting back.

Exchange how you found the experience, as speaker and as listener.

PRACTICE

- In your placement or at work choose an occasion in conversation with a child or young person to use some reflecting back. How does the child respond?

- Use reflecting back in your conversation with an adult when this seems appropriate and notice how this affects your communication.

Reflection: things to discuss or think about

- 'Communication comes naturally to people, there's no need to think about what you do or say.' What do you think about this point of view?

- From what you have learned so far about social pedagogy, do you think that being aware of feedback is important for social pedagogues?

Reflecting back with younger children

Reflecting back can also be used when you're playing with children at times when you want to give a child encouragement and companionship and want to follow the child's lead rather than introduce ideas and games of your own.

'Special times' is the name given to one way of reflecting back, which takes place when you are playing with children. It was developed by Rachel Pinney (1984) as therapy for children with special needs, but the approach can also be used in work with any children, particularly when they need individual attention.

When *special times* is used therapeutically, the adult starts by letting the child know that they are to have a special time together when the child can do whatever he or she wishes. The adult also tells the child that they will make sure that he or she will be in no danger. The adult then pays complete attention to the child, feeding back to them whatever they are doing 'Now you're emptying the box… You want me to hold the teddy,' and so on. Sometimes the feedback is verbal, describing the child's activities in words, but it can also be non-verbal, consisting of smiles, sounds and actions. The play is directed completely by the child and the adult plays whatever part the child wishes, following the child's cues. For example, the child hands the adult a tea cup and the adult has an appreciative drink. The adult does not make any suggestion – or attempt – to take the play further unless the child shows this is required. In this sort of play it would be quite inappropriate for the worker to say 'Can I have a biscuit, as well?' It is quite possible that the child might hand the adult several pretend cups of tea, one after the other and be very pleased with the repetitions. Children use their special times in different ways. The important thing is that they have the total attention and companionship of the adult for this time.

The special times approach can be used sometimes if children seem to need some extra attention. It is especially useful when you want to get to know a child, or just for getting to know a child better. More than anything it means being very attentive to the child, taking on their point of view and, for the time being, sharing their interests rather than imposing your own.

Of course a special times approach is, as the name implies, for special times. It is not always possible to give extended one-to-one time to one particular child. Nevertheless it is useful to be able to communicate with children in this special way, giving them feedback that they are understood and accepted, while at the same time you have the opportunity to understand them better. It is also a corrective to intruding in their play and taking over its direction. If you allow children sometimes to take the lead it is as though they are using you as a very sophisticated plaything. You may be surprised at the length of time for which they are able to sustain their play without any suggestions from you.

PRACTICE

■ Try to find an opportunity to work with a child, reflecting back their play allowing them to take the lead. What happens?

Or:

■ Allow a young child to take you for a walk, round a park. Let them look at things, retrace their steps, linger where they wish, run, or sit down for as long as they like. Just follow where they lead. Only step in if they are going into danger or causing damage.

What do you learn from these exercises about the child and about yourself? How difficult is it to allow the child to take the lead?

Reflection: things to discuss or think about

• Do you think there are any advantages and any disadvantages to working in this way, reflecting back children's play and allowing them to take the lead?

• Can you see any similarities between the labelling that adults carry out when they are interacting with babies (see Chapter 2) and the special times approach described earlier?

OBSERVATION

☐ Watch someone feeding a baby or a toddler, or playing with them. Be on the look-out for the adult following the child's lead and labelling what the child is seeing, hearing, feeling or tasting.

Feedback: key points

- In interpersonal communication 'feedback' passes backwards and forwards between the people who are communicating. Each person reacts, verbally or non-verbally, to the other's communication and each reaction has an effect on the ongoing communication.

- Feedback can let you know if your message is getting through to the other person as you intended or if you need to modify it in some way.

- Listening in an encouraging way gives positive feedback, which encourages a speaker to continue.

- Another form of feedback is reflecting back. To reflect back what someone says you repeat back to them, often in your own words, the content of their message to you. This assures them that they are properly understood. Reflecting back can be especially useful if another person is agitated or shy or if you need to check that you have understood their message.

- A special way of playing with children is to feed back to them, in words, what they are doing, and to follow their lead. This is especially useful for getting to know a child better.

- Related to feedback is when adults 'label' babies' and children's experience for them, giving a name to what they are experiencing.

CHAPTER 6

Reflecting Feelings

Social pedagogues often say that their work uses the whole of themselves: head, hands and heart. This chapter concentrates on the heart: it is about feelings. It is also about, as professionals, being aware of your own feelings, and, as professionals, thinking about them (the head). In other words, it is about developing self-knowledge so that your feelings do not get in the way of what you want to achieve.

In all forms of work with people you are sometimes in close contact with people who are experiencing strong emotions: a teenager in a residential home who is excited to hear that his brother is going to visit him; a child who is delighted because she can at last ride a two-wheeler without stabilisers; a mother who is cross because her child's new coat is missing from the nursery; a mother who phones you from hospital as she anxiously waits for her baby to recover from an anaesthetic; a young person who is upset because he has just been left with a new foster carer and misses his mother. The messages that pass between people are often about personal feelings and need a sensitive response.

What are feelings?

One way of thinking about feelings is as physical sensations and reactions. So if you hear sad news, you may feel a 'lump in your throat' – as the muscles tighten and you find it hard to swallow. Or when you are very anxious – before an exam or an interview, say – you may experience your anxiety as an uneasy crampy feeling in your guts.

Feelings are different from thoughts – although many people mix them up in everyday conversation.

A teacher might say 'What do you feel we should do?' when he is asking for your thoughts, opinions and ideas, not enquiring about emotions. Or a foster carer says 'I feel that teenagers need a good night's sleep' when in fact this is what she *believes* or *thinks* rather than what she feels. At the same time feelings can come into the picture. The carer may feel proud at how she looks after young people, or she may be feeling anxious that she is not doing well enough.

Although thoughts and feelings are different, there are often connections between them, because each can affect the other. If practioners learn that a young person is mistreated at home some may *feel* angry, others depressed. But they do not necessarily act on how they feel; what they *think* about the situation can have a bigger effect on their actions. A playworker who has reason to believe that a child is mistreated, may think to himself 'If I show my feelings, while I am talking to the child's mother, it will make things worse. So I'd better calm down and carry on in a way that is best for the child.' When he reacts in this way his thoughts (his 'head') are controlling his responses, rather than his feelings (his 'heart') and this is a professional social pedagogic response. He would also take appropriate actions such as, in the first instance, discussing his suspicion with a senior worker.

The feelings observed by professionals working on a daily basis with other people are enormously varied. Over a few weeks they might include joy, anger, sadness, affection, friendliness, pride, grief, anger, irritation, trust and worry. In the course of your work it is necessary to be aware of them in other people – children and adults – and in yourself. They can be important messages in their own right; they can also be sources of interference – stopping people from expressing what they want to say or from hearing other people properly (see pp.47–9).

Recognising feelings

Feelings can be expressed both verbally and non-verbally. Someone can tell you 'I feel so happy' when you already know because they are smiling broadly. Here are some of the ways feelings are expressed without words (non-verbally):

- A little girl skips along the pavement.
- A child reaches up and strokes your face.

- A young person smiles hugely, when they sing a song which they have written themselves.
- A friend gives another a hug.
- A mother sighs as she lifts a basket of shopping.
- A father frowns when you tell him you need a cake for the nursery party.
- A child quickly covers her mouth with her hand when you ask 'Who spilt the orange juice?'

These are all signs of emotion which help you to understand something about the other person's feelings. But they are signs only, and do not give you a complete understanding of what is happening. You need to be careful and check out your interpretation in other ways, rather than jumping to conclusions. The frowning father (above) may have just remembered that he's forgotten something for his older child to take for a school sale, or that money is short this week or that his wife is in hospital...he may have a thousand and one reasons for frowning. His frowning does not necessarily mean that he feels hostile towards you or is being uncooperative.

Reflection: things to discuss or think about

- List as many emotions as you can. Some of them may seem very similar to others. Are there any which you are unlikely to meet in the course of your work?
- Which non-verbal behaviour would suggest to you that someone is experiencing the following feelings: depression, worry, affection, glee, fear? (Remember that emotions can be shown on the face, in movement and posture, vocally and by eye contact.)

Responding to feelings

When people who work with children and young people notice someone else's feelings, happy or otherwise, they can respond in different ways. Here are some of them:

1. They may ignore the feelings altogether.

For example, a mother brings her child into the classroom. The mother is hanging her head (perhaps she is crying) and she takes the child's coat off and hands his apple to the teaching assistant without a word. She usually chats. The teaching assistant feels embarrassed. She doesn't know what to say so she keeps quiet and bends down to do up the child's shoe lace, so that she does not have to look at the mother. The mother is desperate to talk about a problem at home, but does not know how to start. She cannot make eye contact with the worker, who is busy with the shoe lace and, after hesitating for a moment, she goes away feeling even worse.

2. They may deny the feelings.

For example, it is Saturday morning in the adventure playground, an hour or so before opening time. Yasmin did not really want to come into work today. A colleague comes in with a bounce in her step and gives her a cheery 'Hello' and begins to sing as she puts the kettle on. Yasmin says 'Oh no, you can't be as cheerful as all that.'

As well as denying cheerful feelings, it is also possible – and perhaps more usual – to deny sad feelings as in the next example. Yasmin is on the way home, feeling really gloomy and her friend calls over from the other side of the street 'Cheer up, it may never happen!'

3. They can also acknowledge the feelings and *reflect them back* and this is what a good social pedagogue would do.

For example, a foster carer is busy with a baby, changing his nappy. Her own 12-year-old comes in from school scowling, slams the door and throws her books down on the table. The carer says 'You look as though you've had a really bad day... I'll be with you in a minute.'

By saying this she communicates that she has picked up something of what her daughter is feeling and that she accepts this. Acknowledging and reflecting back emotions shows respect for what another person is experiencing; in other words it shows respect for the person, in keeping with the values of social pedagogy. If a child comes crying to you with a cut knee, 'You've cut your knee and it hurts badly' is one appropriate response as you start to take action. It reflects back what has happened and what the child is feeling about it – you are letting him know that you understand and accept him. Being accepted is an important experience for children which helps them to feel secure and confident about themselves.

It is important to acknowledge children's feelings and not deny them

Some people might object that it would be better to try to cheer up a hurt child or to tell him that his knee 'doesn't hurt that much'. This would be to deny the child's own feelings. I have noticed that when adults deny that children are upset, they often cry all the louder – as though to convince their listeners of how bad they feel, to get through to them that this is really important and needs attention. It is also true that if children are constantly made to feel ashamed of crying, they come to believe that sharing painful feelings is not permitted and may well carry this understanding into adult life. If you acknowledge and reflect their feelings, they are comforted and know that you share their understanding of the situation.

Partings

Sad or angry feelings are frequently displayed at times involving partings, when children are put in the care of someone they do not know very well. In early years work partings must be handled with sensitivity. If at all possible there should be a period of time for settling in. Children need to get used to new adults, to being one of a group of children, to having a routine which is different from home and to being in an unfamiliar setting with strange furniture and unfamiliar toys.

A gradual approach is probably the best for settling in. With nurseries and childminders, there should be short visits with one or other parent. Because the parent is present, children feel secure getting to know you and their new surroundings. During these first visits you can start by just watching the parent taking care of the child – taking their coat off, taking them to the toilet, helping them to wash their hands. Then gradually you can take over some of this while the parent is present and now watching you. In this way children see that their parents trust you. You can use this time to find out more about children.

You will find out some of this from the children themselves, depending on their age and the circumstances. You need to know about their likes and dislikes with regard to food and other parts of their daily routine. Are there people at home, or pets, whom they might refer to? What does the child or young person call them? This is necessary for understanding what a child is talking about. Are there special words or signs they use for going to the toilet? Have they got any comfort object, like a teddy or piece of blanket which they turn to in distress? What do they call it? It may be useful to make a written record of this sort of information, so that it is there for other professionals who may work with the child and as a reminder for yourself.

All of this knowledge will help your communications with the child, so that you will be in a better position to receive their messages and to understand their point of view – how do they see their world? And because they have had time to get used to you, the child will be in a better position to understand you.

On the first occasion when a parent goes away, they should leave the child for a few minutes only, letting them know that they will return soon. They can, over a few days, increase the time they are away.

Even when these gradual steps are taken, some children are still upset when their parents leave. In other cases an emergency of some sort may mean that children are left with strange carers, without any preparation at all. When, for whatever reason, children are upset at parting you should acknowledge how they feel, as well as reassuring them that their parents will be back later. They may want to cling to you during the first days of separation and, as far as possible, you should allow this and make use of the opportunity to get to know them better. They will gain security as they come to realise that you understand them, accept them – feelings and all – and respond to them when they need you. When this happens, they will be ready to venture away from you and find interesting games and playmates, knowing that you are at hand.

Finding out about the children who are being left in your care is essential. Residential care staff and foster carers have to build up this knowledge more slowly, often directly from the child or young person themselves. At the same time they should avoid bombarding the child with too many questions: they need to find a balance between showing interest and being over-inquisitive (see Chapter 8).

Reflecting adults' feelings

Sensitive communication also involves awareness of adults' feelings, as well as those of children, and the ability and willingness to reflect them. You may need to show someone – an angry colleague or an upset father – that you know something of their experience by reflecting their feelings back to them. So if someone says 'I'm going to see my mother tonight…' and sighs deeply, replying 'You're not feeling too good about it' communicates that you have picked up an important message. You are reflecting *feelings* back to the speaker. This is different from reflecting back *content*, which was discussed in Chapter 5.

To take the above example again, if someone says, sighing deeply, 'I'm going to see my mother tonight…', and you respond cheerfully: 'So you're off to Manchester' (where her mother lives), ignoring the sigh, then you are ignoring the *feelings* behind what is said and reflecting only the *content* of the words. This is probably not an adequate response for the other person. It is necessary to accept that the other person feels as they do – even if you think that their feelings are unrealistic. For example if a mother seems over-anxious about the possibility that her child has got chicken pox, it does not help her to say 'You're worried in case he's got chicken pox!' in a tone of complete scorn, suggesting that she is stupid to let such a trivial matter upset her. If the mother is extremely anxious you should first show that you understand and accept how she is feeling. You may then want to provide some realistic information – for example that chicken pox is unpleasant, but not dangerous, for a five-year-old.

In providing feedback, go carefully, in case you have misunderstood, or have over-estimated how the other person is feeling. For example, say 'You look a bit down,' rather than 'You look totally devastated'; 'You're worried in case he's got chicken pox,' rather than 'You're feeling terribly anxious about it.'

In some circumstances you may feel that acknowledging someone's feelings would leave you out of your depth. You could believe that it would be difficult to handle the situation if the other person were to say more about what was troubling them, for example if you came to believe that a mother was trying to confide in you that her child was being abused. In cases like this, and if you think that the situation is serious for the child who is involved, it may be better to let a senior colleague know what is happening and let them deal with the situation, rather than trying to handle it yourself. (Disclosing private information is discussed in Chapter 13.)

In summary, if you want to encourage the process of communication, which includes the communication of feelings, try to see things from the other person's point of view, accept their messages and let them know that you accept them. This may not come easily to start with but practice helps. Reflecting feelings relates to social pedagogy in many ways:

- It requires staff to use head, hands and heart in a professional way.

- It is a means of assuring the other person that you understand and accept their feelings and so on, building a trusting relationship.

- It is a practice that helps you to get in touch with other people's perspective on life, and to see the world through their eyes.

Reflection: things to discuss or think about

- Have you ever had the experience of someone ignoring your feelings? Has anyone ever denied your feelings? Have you ever noticed either of these things happening to somebody else? What was the reaction?

- Are there any problems around acknowledging other people's feelings in your work? Are there any disadvantages if you do not acknowledge the feelings of others?

Exercise: reflecting back feelings

- Practise reflecting back feelings with another person. Think of some problem you have in your work or training, which you are willing to share with someone else.

- Find a partner and each take turns, for about five minutes, to share your problem. When you are the speaker remember to stop to give the other person chance to reflect back. The listener should reflect back feelings and use encouraging listening.

- Then change roles so that each person has a turn to be listener and speaker.

- After you have each had a turn share with each other how you found the experience – being a listener and being listened to. Were there any learning points?

PRACTICE

- If suitable opportunities arise, practise reflecting back feelings in your communications with adults and with children or young people.

- Notice what happens: how are the feelings communicated to you; how does the other person respond when you reflect back? Are you satisfied with how you handle things?

OBSERVATION

☐ Watch a television play or soap opera and follow one of the main characters.

☐ What feelings does the character communicate?

☐ How do other people react to the feelings?

☐ Are the feelings accepted, reflected back, denied or ignored?

Sad events in children's lives

Sooner or later in working with children and young people, staff come across children who are upset because of something that happens in their family, perhaps the loss of a parent through illness, death or marriage breakdown. Staff find this painful. They are aware that they cannot change things for the child and there is the possibility that they are reminded of sad events from their own past. In such circumstances, a professional stance is to acknowledge – to yourself – that your own feelings are involved in how you may interact with the child or young person concerned and to communicate with them in such a way that their interests are best served. Danish social pedagogues talk about 'having room in your heart' for the people you work with (Petrie *et al.* 2006). This is an important concept. It means that, as a professional, you are ready to accept other people and their experience of life, even when your own view of the world is very different, or their experience arouses painful memories and feelings for you. As we saw earlier, acceptance, conveyed by sensitive and appropriate responses, is a way of building attachment and trust.

Because of their own painful feelings, some staff may try to avoid any communication the child attempts about the sad experience. This is unwise: if young people are already feeling sad, or anxious, or angry, to deny their feelings by ignoring them or 'brushing them under the carpet' may make children confused, thus adding to their unhappiness. Accepting their feelings, and letting them know that you do so, is more helpful to them. This is not to suggest that you actively raise painful subjects – although sometimes you may have to do so – but when they do so themselves, you should accept their experience, whether this is conveyed in words or in other ways.

Sometimes children and young people ask questions about subjects like death or illness which you do not know how to deal with. They may make you feel anxious because you are not sure if they are mature enough to understand or to cope with the answer. It is always best to answer these sorts of questions in a straightforward way. If you do not do so, you run the risk of confusing children. You can also make them more fearful if they suspect that the answer to their question must be devastating, because you keep it from them. In cases such as these, answer quite simply and truthfully and be ready to answer any further questions that arise (see also pp.99–102).

You may find that in the course of your work you become quite involved in the events of a child's life and in their feelings, and that this involvement is difficult to bear. If this happens, talking things over with an attentive colleague or a more senior member of staff can help you to sort out and accept your own feelings about the situation. It is then easier to give the child the acceptance and support which they need.

Reflection: things to discuss or think about

1. At a youthclub attended by young people with disabilities, a girl died. A few months after her death there was a special ceremony of remembrance for her. Children and staff planted a tree together, spoke about the girl who had died and thought about her. The young people had made decorations which they hung on the tree during the ceremony.

    What do you think about this approach? How would you have felt as a member of staff? Should disabled young people be treated differently when it comes to talking to them about death and other sad events? Do you think that it would be appropriate to have a memorial ceremony in a nursery? In a residential care home? In a foster home? For a member of staff? For a child? For a teenager? What lies behind your answers?

2. You are a childminder. A child you've looked after for two years dies. The other children ask about her. Do you reply:

   • 'No more questions, just get on with your dinner' *or*

   • 'Tracy's mum has moved and Tracy won't be coming back any more' *or*

   • 'Tracy was ill and died.'

   Take each answer in turn, what problems do you see arising from each answer? What advantages do you see?
   Is there a better answer? What would you say?

3. You are a playworker. Gary comes up to you, beaming, and says: 'My dad's coming out of prison tomorrow.' (You did not know he was in prison.) Do you reply:

   • 'Oh, isn't that lovely' *or*

   • 'Don't tell stories' *or*

   • 'Would you like to play football tonight?' (or some equivalent)

   • Or do you make some other reply? Why do you make this choice?

OBSERVATION

☐ Spend some time observing children or young people and pay special attention to their feelings.

☐ What feelings do you think you observe?

☐ How do you recognise these feelings – through words, body language, tone of voice?

☐ Do you think that the feelings are accepted, denied or ignored by adults and by other children or young people?

Reflecting feelings: key points

- Social pedagogues sometimes speak of working with the head, hands and heart. Feelings relate to the heart – but professional workers need to use both their heads and their hearts, to respond sensitively to other people.

- Feelings play a large part in interpersonal communication so be alert for the messages – verbal or non-verbal – that people, of whatever age, provide about their feelings. Be observant.

- In interpersonal communication in your place of work it is appropriate, often, to give feedback about other people's feelings, that is to identify the feelings and reflect them back to the other person. This shows that you accept the other person and their experience – your heart has room enough for them.

- Do not ignore or deny other people's feelings.

- Be aware of your own feelings and how they may affect your communication with other people.

- If a situation which involves feelings seems serious, and you do not feel confident about handling it yourself, let a senior colleague know.

- Answer questions about sad or painful subjects as simply and directly as you can.

CHAPTER 7

Communications About Yourself

So far we have concentrated on feedback and especially on the encouraging, positive responses you can give to help people to communicate well when they are talking about themselves and their concerns. But there are also occasions in this sort of work when it is appropriate to talk about yourself, personally, as well as about any professional concerns. When you tell another person something about yourself which they did not know before, you are making a *disclosure*, although the term 'disclosure' is often reserved for fairly serious matters. People often talk to family and friends about personal matters. You tell them what sort of a day you have had, how you are feeling, what you are looking forward to. You may talk about important things that have happened in the past or problems you are having at present, but often people communicate about less serious matters. It is good to be open, to share experience and this goes for work as well as home.

Professional, personal and private communications

Social pedagogy makes a distinction between three concepts that each begins with P: the professional, the personal and the private. It is useful to understand the difference between these concepts, especially in working situations.

Professional communications

Professionals are aware of their responsibilities towards the children, young people, colleagues, parents and others with whom they work and use their knowledge and skills to carry out these responsibilities in the best way they can. Their interactions with other people are conducted on a professional basis.

Personal communications

There are many occupations in which being personal is not a priority. For example, for a computer technician little of their work is at a personal level. There are also professionals, such as those in some medical occupations who, while they work with people, have much less opportunity for more personal communication – it is not that they treat other people as objects, but that it is less appropriate for them to communicate about themselves.

However, for staff engaged in 'people work', the professional and the personal go hand in hand. They are not merely skilled at following procedures, applying techniques and reflecting on theory. Just as the social pedagogue is concerned with the whole child, they also bring themselves as whole persons to their work: people with personal as well as professional experience, fellow human beings with feelings, hopes, fears and humour.

Private communications

Of course you do not want to share everything with everyone. You may feel comfortable telling a close friend about something which you would not tell to others. You can probably remember keeping information to yourself – not because you were being secretive but because you decided that this was not the appropriate person, or perhaps the appropriate time, for sharing.

Often you make these choices almost instinctively, without having to think very much about them. However, there are times when you need to make decisions about any self-disclosure you might make at work. This is because, as well as being a normal part of communication, some types of self-disclosure may stand in the way of what you are trying to achieve in your work – your professional responsibilities.

You may, therefore, have to consider when and to whom you make disclosures about yourself, and what to disclose.

When disclosure is helpful

Here are some points to help you decide if self-disclosure is helpful.

Is the information appropriate? Some personal information is more weighty, more serious, than other personal information; disclosing serious information about yourself may be inappropriate, as the following contrasting examples show.

1. A worker is talking to a young person. She says 'You went to the seaside on Saturday? I went to the seaside too – we went to Marshbanks.'

2. A nursery teacher says to a mother 'I forgot to take my anti-depressant this morning and everything is getting me down!'

In the first example the worker makes a disclosure about herself. She tells the young person what she did on Saturday and this personal disclosure could be the beginning of an interesting conversation. I leave you to imagine some of the possible consequences of the second, highly unlikely, example! However, it points to an important lesson: the more serious or weighty the disclosure, the more there is a question about its appropriateness. In this kind of work, serious personal information is not for sharing without good reason. (Notice this is not to say that serious material must *never* be shared, but that there must be an equally serious reason for doing so.)

Disclosure can make for closeness

Talking about yourself makes you less distant and may help another person to feel ready to share their experience with you. Perhaps you need to encourage a shy person, so that you can get to know each other better, and talking a little about your own experience is one way to do this. We shall see in the next chapter that asking a series of questions, which is sometimes used to encourage conversation, may in fact make conversation more difficult.

For example: you are sitting next to a volunteer helping on a coach trip. The volunteer is new to the group and seems to be rather shy.

One way in which you can help her feel more at ease is to give her the opportunity to talk about herself. Saying something about yourself like 'This reminds me of school trips when I was little...' could start the ball rolling. This is not the same as 'hogging the conversation', as long as you leave space for her to join in.

There is also a place for sharing your own experience in your conversations with the children or young people who you work with. You can foster communication by saying something about yourself – your experience, feelings and thoughts. This can be more effective in helping the conversation along than a stream of questions (see Chapter 8). It can also introduce interesting subjects which stretch children's understanding and widen their horizons.

Reflection: things to discuss or think about

- Can you remember interesting adults you knew when you were younger? What sorts of things did they tell you about?

- Did they have any belongings, any special objects, that seemed to arouse your curiosity and lead into an interesting conversation – photographs or other treasures? Bearing in mind the age group you work with, is there any way that you could use some of your own personal belongings – things you take out of your pocket or handbag – to start conversations? Is there anything you could bring from home which might interest them?

- In your experience, is it easier to make conversation (not just a set of questions and answers) with children or with adults?

Sharing experience can show understanding

By talking about your own experience it is possible to show that you understand the other person's problem. A teacher says to a mother: 'He's still waking you up during the night? I had the same with mine

– I used to long for six hours undisturbed sleep.' The mother knows that the teacher appreciates her situation.

Remember, though, that the experiences of two people which on the surface sound alike, may in fact be very different. You may not really understand the feelings of another person in a difficult situation, even though you have lived through something that seems similar yourself. For example the feelings involved in one divorce may be totally unlike those involved in another. Do not, therefore, claim that you fully understand what is happening to somebody else, on the grounds that you have been through it yourself. Be ready to listen.

When disclosure is unhelpful

Disclosure can be a burden to others

Sharing your private problems may mean burdening other people with them. This may be acceptable between close friends, but it is not appropriate when your relationship is a professional one. At work, your job is to be of service to the children and their families; they have no similar obligations towards you.

Similarly, talking about yourself can shift the focus of a conversation to your interests, at a point when this may not be useful. If a mother wants to talk to you about her teenager and the problems she has getting her to do her homework, telling her how your niece, of the same age, is now getting on well at school would be a distraction. It would suggest that you are not interested in the difficulties which the mother is experiencing. There are many times in your work, as we saw earlier, when encouraging listening and reflecting back are the most useful responses rather than disclosing information about yourself.

Taking too large a part in the conversation

Sometimes people take too large a part in the conversation, talking a great deal about themselves without allowing other people a chance to contribute. This is boring for others and may lead them to feel under-valued by the person concerned. This goes against the aims of social pedagogy which sets out to value other people and build their self-confidence. Sometimes people working with the youngest children feel that they have to keep up a stream of talk with children, because they have heard that this is the way to encourage them to develop language. Taking turns is also important, and space should be left for the children's share in conversation, using the ways covered in earlier chapters.

Friends or friendly?

Some personal statements may suggest that you see yourself as a *friend*, rather than *friendly*. It is important to be clear about your relationship with people you meet at work. There is a difference between your relationship with friends and that which you have with parents and colleagues. You choose your friends, but not the people you meet professionally. Friends have a fairly equal relationship based on liking to be with one another, but you do not choose the colleagues, parents and children you work with.

Sometimes, even, you may find yourself working with people you do not really like. Personal friendships can develop at work but working relationships focus primarily on the well-being of children and parents and on co-operating with colleagues. Behaving differently with different parents or children, by disclosing more about yourself to some than to others, suggests that you prefer some over others, that you have favourites. This can lead to others feeling excluded and to the suggestion that there are 'cliques'. This is not to say that 'friendliness' – sensitivity, encouragement, warmth – is out of place, in fact it is essential, but friendliness should, to the best of your ability, be shown equally to all the people you work with.

Reflection: things to discuss or think about

1. Bearing in mind what you have just read, how appropriate would it be for someone to say to a parent:

   - 'Monday again, I didn't feel like coming into work this morning.'

   - 'I'm going to be away for a couple of weeks because I'm getting married.'

- 'I spent most of the weekend working for the local Labour/Conservative/Liberal Democratic Party.'

- 'I know how you are feeling, my own partner died last year.'

- I'm at my wits end about my father; I feel I ought to stay at home to look after him, but I need to work for the money.'

- 'I'm feeling great today!'

Which was the most difficult statement to decide about? Why? Would you decide differently if the same remarks were made to a colleague?

2. 'You can't make rules about self-disclosure – it depends on the work you're doing and where you're working: if you're a residential care worker, a childminder, a nursery officer in a hospital, a playworker in an after-school scheme or whatever.' What do you think about this statement?

3. 'You can be friends with the parents and you can be friends with your colleagues.' What do you think about this point of view?

4. What reasons can you think of for and against nursery workers wearing political badges or religious symbols, which could be seen as an act of disclosure?

5. Should you ever talk to parents or children about any difficulties you are having with colleagues?

OBSERVATION

☐ Become aware of the part of self-disclosure in people's conversation. Listen at work and elsewhere, wherever you are. Or watch a play or soap opera on television and for quarter of an hour concentrate on one character. Does the character use encouraging listening, reflecting back, questions or disclosure? One more than the other or equally?

☐ Was there anything you specially noticed about the part that self-disclosure plays in communication? How common is it? Do you notice conversations where there is little self-disclosure from either party? What are these conversations like?

Communicating about yourself: key points

- Social pedagogy distinguishes between professional, personal and private forms of interpersonal communication.

- For staff engaged in 'people work', the professional and the personal go hand in hand. They bring themselves as whole beings to their work: with personal as well as professional experience.

- Personal self-disclosure gives other people information about yourself which they would not otherwise have.

- Personal self-disclosure on your part can encourage others to communicate with you, it makes you more approachable.

- Self-disclosure also has disadvantages. It can burden other people with your problems; change the focus from the other person to yourself; suggest that you are a 'friend' rather than 'friendly'; suggest 'favouritism' if you disclose more to some people than to others.

- Disclosing something about your own experience may suggest that you understand and sympathise with another person's situation. But be careful as this may be misleading; no two experiences are the same.

- Learn to distinguish what should be kept private and is not appropriate in work situations.

CHAPTER 8

Questions

Skilled interpersonal communication involves many activities such as: observing and listening, avoiding interference, reflecting back and talking about yourself, your feelings, ideas and experience. This chapter introduces asking *questions*. This is a very familiar activity but we are not always aware of the effect that different sorts of questions can have in communicating with other people. Sometimes they help the process along but at other times they get in the way. Social pedagogy reminds us of the importance of being aware of how different forms of communication can affect others and this applies to the use of questions. Being attentive to other people's questions and answering as best we can is a means of respect, while asking questions is a way of learning how the world looks to somebody else. As we saw earlier, social pedagogues try to understand where another person is coming from in order to work effectively with them and to acknowledge different understandings.

Open questions and closed questions

Asking questions well is an art in itself – think of a good radio interview compared with one that goes badly. An experienced interviewer just seems to start a conversation going with a simple question then guides it along with further questions, drawing out the experience of the interviewed person. Other interviewers can shut someone up with a stream of questions which get answered briefly or in monosyllables. Choosing the right type of question can be vital for obtaining full information from the interviewee. A useful way of grouping questions is according to whether they are *closed* or *open*.

Closed questions

These are questions which can be answered fairly simply, often with the words 'Yes' or 'No', or with an answer which is short and limited. For example:

- Did you enjoy the film?
- You've drawn a house, haven't you?
- Is that a pussy cat?
- Do you like mushrooms?
- Have you heard their new album?
- Would you like the red cup or the blue one?

The above questions are all *closed* questions and answers to them may very well consist of only one word: 'Yes', 'No', 'Red' or 'Blue'. If in your work you ask mainly closed questions, someone who is feeling shy – a child, a parent or new member of staff – may answer with only one word and then it is up to you, once again, to continue the conversation. When you ask closed questions you are taking control of the interaction, which becomes information-gathering rather than conversation. Unless the other person is quite assertive, it is not easy for them to make their contribution or to introduce subjects they are interested in.

Open questions

Open questions on the other hand, give the person you are talking to much more choice in how they answer.

They often begin with either 'How' or 'Why':

- Why did you want to see me?
- How did you get the icing smooth, like that?
- How does the new flat compare with where you were before?
- How do you feel about that?
- What happens when you remind her to do her homework?

The person answering is never limited to 'Yes ' or 'No' with open questions; they are given the opportunity to provide longer answers, bringing in additional information and opinions if they wish to do so. This does not mean that you should never use closed questions. They are useful for clarification for example 'Did you mean that the window was open all night?' checks that the questioner has understood the situation properly. They are also used for obtaining simple information as in 'How old is he?' But open questions are better than closed questions if you want to encourage someone to talk about their experience.

'How' or 'Why'?

Questions that begin with 'How' are somehow less threatening than those that begin with 'Why'. You may notice a small difference in feeling between 'Why did you send her to nursery?' and 'How did you come to send her to nursery?' The first question asks for reasons and a timid person might feel that there is the risk of giving a wrong answer. 'How did you come to send her to nursery?' on the other hand, is asking about someone's experience, the events that led to a decision, and may seem less threatening.

Exercise: 20 questions

- Find a partner and each write down the name of a child or young person you work with. You each have 20 questions to find out as much as possible about their partner's child: their background, age, gender, likes and dislikes, what sort of child they are. The only answers allowed are 'Yes' or 'No' so questions must be framed accordingly – that is, they must be closed questions.

- When you have each had a turn, try the exercise again. This time you are both allowed to use open questions.

- What differences did you notice between the two exercises – as a questioner and as someone providing answers. How did you feel? Did open questions or closed questions give you a better picture of the person concerned?

Helpful questions

Questions can make space for others to talk. Short questions of this sort, tagged on to the end of statements, are often used to indicate to others that it is their turn to join in a conversation. They are called 'tag' questions. 'It was a good film, wasn't it?' you ask or, after giving your opinion, 'You know what I mean?'

Sometimes questions are used to reflect back. Someone says 'I really like working in the Assessment Unit' and her friend answers with a question which reflects back what has just been said – 'You're enjoying it then?' – at which point the first speaker has permission to continue talking about her experience. Or a worker can use a short question just to keep a child talking. 'I went out with my mum,' says the child. 'Did you?' asks the worker, showing interest. 'Yes, and we saw our Nan,' continues the child, encouraged by the question.

Questions can make things clear

Sometimes you need to ask questions to clarify a situation because something is not clear, you don't understand or you need extra information. Occasionally people are diffident about this and are afraid to ask about something in case they look foolish. This is an attitude which can lead to difficulties and confusion.

Questions show you're interested

Questions, especially open questions, can show that you have a friendly interest in someone. If there are not too many questions, they help the other person to relax and talk more easily about themselves. 'Where did you go for your holiday? What was it like?' may start the ball rolling.

Questions needing care
Too many questions

Although questions can show that you are interested in another person, asking too many questions is daunting for the other person. So you need to be ready to use other communication skills if you find yourself in a conversation which seems to be getting stuck. For example you can say something about your own experience like 'I can never manage to do the icing so I get my friend to do it for me', followed by another question if necessary: 'How did you learn to do it?' Or you can use reflecting back: 'You really enjoy doing it,' and wait for an answer.

Too many questions can put an end to communication

Sensitive questions

We have all, at some time or other, met people who ask questions about things which are none of their business, questions which touch on sensitive areas and which give rise to resentment. In most work with children and young people, questions about another person's private life are not necessary and should not arise. But sometimes senior workers need to ask sensitive questions in order to clarify a situation.

For example, it may seem from something a father has said that a child's mother has left home. A worker may decide to clarify this with a question 'I don't know if I got it right, but is Emma's mother not living with you and Emma now?' If the father wished to convey this information, then it is important for the worker to know about it, and their question is justifiable.

Nevertheless sensitive questions can be threatening and intrusive. Before asking a question which is at all sensitive ask yourself:

- Is it essential for me to find out about this?
- Do I really need to know for the good of the child and in order to carry out my professional duties?
- Am I the right person to be asking this question?
- Would it perhaps be better to talk to a senior worker about any anxiety I have about the child's welfare?

Asking questions carries the responsibility for using the resultant information for the good of the child. If, to take an extreme example, as a result of your questions, someone confides that another adult in the family is abusing a child, then it is your responsibility to pass the information on to a senior colleague. If you are working as a childminder you should speak to a local authority adviser, or if you are a foster carer you should speak to the child's social worker. You should also tell the person who gave you the information that you are going to pass it on (see p.165).

Reflection: things to discuss or think about

- Two playworkers are talking over a coffee. One says to the other 'I'd never ask parents questions about their private lives, no matter what I thought was happening.' The other replies 'Well, I think I would if I had to. But with children it's different. You should never ask children questions about their families.'
- What would you say if you joined in the conversation? What reasons would you give?

OBSERVATION

- ☐ Become aware of the part questions play in interpersonal communication in everyday life. Do questions seem to help a conversation along or put a stop to it?

☐ Watch some interviews on television, or listen to interviews on the radio. Does the interviewer use open or closed questions? Are there any questions which seem to threaten the interviewee? Do you notice any differences between interviewers?

Asking children questions

Asking questions has been an educational method used for thousands of years. As we have seen, some questions are encouraging and they can help people to take part in communication. Careful questions can lead them to make discoveries for themselves and draw their attention to different aspects of a problem. Another reason for asking questions is to find out what someone knows or how much they understand, for example asking young children questions about colour, number or size. But asking children certain sorts of questions can become a habit without any real purpose. For example in nursery work a member of staff might say 'What a nice house. What colour is it?' Stock questions like 'What colour is it?' may be no more than paying the child a little verbal attention in passing, especially if the member of staff is not really interested in whether the child can recognise colours.

On the other hand, labelling and reflecting back (see p.36 and p.65) give children information, show that you are taking in what they are doing or noticing and encourage them to speak. So saying something like 'You've painted it green, except for this red bit here, haven't you?' keeps the conversation focused on the child's own activities and leaves space for their contribution to the conversation.

Reflection: things to discuss or think about

• Can you remember teachers asking questions when you were at school?

• How did you feel when you were asked questions?

• What are the disadvantages, in your experience, connected with asking children questions?

Children and young people's questions

Children can be persistent questioners when they need information for their own purposes and especially when they are puzzled – when something does not make sense according to their present understanding of the world.

These persistent questions can often be difficult for staff because they do not know the answer to questions like 'Why doesn't the fly fall off the ceiling?' Or staff can be puzzled by a child's question because they cannot see the world from the child's point of view, they do not fully understand how the child makes sense of the world, or what perplexes them. Often they may not know enough about the children's lives to make sense of what they say.

It is worthwhile to be patient with persistent questions so as to discover what it is, exactly, that is puzzling them. Trying to understand a child's or young person's point of view and providing the required information is a valuable interaction, a way in which children can find out about the world, expand their knowledge and put right their own misunderstandings.

Exercise: a child's questions

Read the following conversation, which was recorded in real life and comes from an interesting book by Barbara Tizard and Martin Hughes (2002, pp.95–97). Pay special attention to the child's questions:

GIRL: What did Pamela say?

MOTHER: She's having to pay everybody else's bills for the window cleaner, 'cause they're all out.

GIRL: Why are they all out?

MOTHER: 'Cause they're working or something.

GIRL: Aren't they silly!

MOTHER: Well, you have to work to earn money, don't you?

GIRL: Yeah…if they know what day the window cleaner comes, they should stay here.

MOTHER: They should stay at home? Well, I don't know, they can't always...

(At this point there is a change in the conversation, but the girl raises the subject again, later.)

GIRL: Mummy?

MOTHER: Mmm.

GIRL: Umm...she can't pay everybody's, er...all the bills to the window cleaner, can she?

MOTHER: No, she can't pay everybody's bills...she sometimes pays mine if I'm out.

GIRL: 'Cause it's fair.

MOTHER: Mmm, it is.

GIRL: Umm, where does she leave the money?

MOTHER: She doesn't leave it anywhere, she hands it to the window cleaner when he's finished.

GIRL: And then she gives it to us?

MOTHER: No, no, she doesn't have to pay us.

GIRL: Then the window cleaner gives it to us?

MOTHER: No, we give the window cleaner money, he does work for us, and we have to give him money.

GIRL: Why?

MOTHER: Well, because he's been working for us cleaning our windows. He doesn't do it for nothing.

GIRL: Why do you have money if you have...if people clean your windows?

MOTHER: Well, the window cleaner needs money, doesn't he?

GIRL: Why?

MOTHER: To buy clothes for his children and food for them to eat.

GIRL: Well, sometimes window cleaners don't have children.

MOTHER: Quite often they do.

GIRL: And something on his own to eat, and for curtains?

MOTHER: And for paying his gas bills and electricity bill and for paying for petrol for his car. All sorts of things you have to pay for, you see. You have to earn money somehow, and he earns it by cleaning other people's windows and big shop windows and things.

GIRL: And the person who got the money gives it to people...

- What misunderstandings or puzzles does the girl have?
- What information does she acquire?
- What part does the mother play in helping her to learn?
- How useful do you think conversations like these are in developing children's understanding?

This sequence was between a mother and child at home. This is what happened when some children and young people went for a walk by the river with their playworker.

In answer to the children's questions, the playworker told them about the different types of water fowl and about their colouring. One child was confused because both ducks and drakes were called ducks. The playworker discussed this. She also told the children that a female swan was called a pen. They talked about how the swans would make their way up river, all the way to the next town. The children asked whether they would fly or swim. The playworker answered their questions. They went further along the bank to the weir, and stopped to watch its commotion for about ten minutes. Again there was much conversation about it, and questions from the children. One child asked about a tributary river that could be seen coming in on the further bank. The playworker told him its name and explained how smaller rivers and streams fed into the larger rivers which then fed into the sea.

(Petrie 1994, p.108)

OBSERVATION

☐ Over the next few weeks, be on the look-out for children's questions: single questions or sequences of questions, when a child is determined to find out more or to get at the root of something. If you are involved answer patiently without changing the subject.

☐ Describe any sequence of questions that you find interesting.

☐ Say what lies behind the children's questions – what lack of understanding or need for information.

☐ Include any difficulties you have in understanding what lies behind the questions – your own puzzlement.

Exercise: questions to help communication

Read the following conversation and examine the nursery worker's questions. Do they help the child to communicate? Can you suggest other things that the worker could have said?

A four-year-old boy is looking at a picture of a rabbit looking at a newspaper. He tells his friend that it is a mouse.

NURSERY WORKER: It isn't a mouse actually. Do you know what it is?

BOY: (*no answer*)

NURSERY WORKER: Do you know how they make a warren?

BOY: What's their name?

NURSERY WORKER: They don't have names, they're just rabbits. Does your daddy read newspapers?

BOY: I've got lots of books.

NURSERY WORKER: Does he read them to you?

BOY: Depends.

NURSERY WORKER: What books does he read to you?

BOY: My brother's name is Ian.

NURSERY WORKER: Put the book away when you've finished.

OBSERVATION

☐ Observe an adult interacting with children or young people, individually or in a group of children. A meal time could be a good time to choose.

☐ Notice what part, if any, questions play. What sort of questions are asked (open questions, closed questions, 'tag' questions (see pp.92–7)?

☐ How does the child (or children) respond to questions?

☐ Do they seem to help the child take part in the conversation?

Questions: key points

- In conversations with other people of whatever age, questions can help communication or they can get in the way.

- Closed questions usually need one-word answers, for example 'Yes' or 'No', and leave little space for the other person to make a contribution.

- Open questions often begin with 'Why' or 'How', giving the other person much more scope for answering at greater length.

- Some questions, known as 'tag' questions, are not real questions, they are just a way of indicating that you have finished your turn in the conversation. They include phrases like 'Isn't it?' and 'You know?'

- Questions can be used for clarification when you are not sure about something.

- Questions can show that you have a friendly interest in someone.

- Too many questions and insensitive questions are intrusive.

- With children and young people save questions for when you really need to know the answer, for example to carry on your conversation, or if you need to find out what they know. Otherwise be sparing in asking questions and if you ask them listen to the answers.

- Children and young people can ask questions persistently when they are in search of knowledge; be patient, try to understand what they want to know and give them information.

CHAPTER 9

Messages About Power and Messages About Equality

Throughout society there are groups and individuals who by their actions, including their interpersonal communications, exert power over others. The messages they give to others, about their own superiority and other people's low status, are sometimes quite open but sometimes rather hidden. In either case the messages convey disrespect. Those involved may be aware of what they are doing but at other times they don't understand the sort of messages their communications carry. The subject of this chapter is how interpersonal communications can be used to control others and deny them equality and respect. It is also about how to be aware of this in order to prevent it happening.

The chapter starts with interpersonal communication which is openly controlling. Next we examine other, sometimes less direct, controlling messages which result in and sustain social inequality between people: men and women, different ethnic groups, disabled people, gay men and lesbians, young and old, rich and poor, and other groups.

Open control

There are times at work when you have to let other people know what is 'acceptable' behaviour and what the boundaries rules are. Chapter 11 will suggest how to do this constructively, not by seeking to *control* others but by treating them with respect, trying to see their point of view and seeking reasonable solutions to problems together.

Sometimes people try to control others, quite openly, by threats, by force, by blaming them and moralising about them. In such controlling communications the spoken message is 'Do what I say' together with other messages, spoken and unspoken, which suggest that one person is more important – wiser, stronger or simply more powerful than the other. It is these *controlling* messages which we consider first. These are oppressive communications which express an individual's power, or wish for power over others, and which are destructive of other people's self-esteem. For social pedagogues, harming a child's self-esteem is seriously wrong. When a member of staff is disparaging to a child, the child feels insignificant and silly. Being judgemental about someone or moralising about them is disrespectful and this is a message which gets through. Also the feelings aroused can cause *interference* (see p.47), so the listener may block out part of the intended message and only hear the part that is hurtful.

The following statements all seek to control people and put them down:

- 'I would never have done it like that. Why didn't you ask me first?' (Here the speaker claims superiority and the other person feels stupid or angry or both.)

- 'It's so lazy, leaving everything lying about. Always clear up before the children start their meal.' (The implication of this is that the speaker is hard working, well organised and morally superior to the other person.)

- 'How can she eat her dinner – when you've filled her up with biscuits?' (Meaning 'You don't know as much about looking after children as I do – or perhaps you just don't care.')

- 'Your problem is that you don't listen.' (With the implication that the other person is insensitive, incompetent and stubborn.)

- 'Waste not want not – you should never have thrown it away, we could have used it today.' (Pointing out a moral lesson and blaming the other person at the same time.)

In all of these examples the speaker is trying to control someone. They use language and expressions that hurt, taking no account of the other's feelings and self-esteem. Their strongest message is that the speaker disapproves of the other.

Controlling messages can be destructive and hurtful

To take another example, this time where the control message may seem less obvious, a member of staff in a nursery notices that a mother who is changing her young baby is not managing very well. She takes the nappy from the mother with a sigh and says 'I showed you the easiest way to do that this morning!' Here, by reminding the mother that she had been given a demonstration earlier, the worker 'puts the mother down'. An important part of the message is that the mother is inexperienced, and rather silly into the bargain. This sort of communication can only be harmful. First, it may damage the mother's self-confidence in looking after her baby. Second, it harms the relationship – which should be one of warmth and trust – between the mother and the member of staff. One of the principles of social pedagogy is to value the contributions of colleagues and others, and to work as a team. This is a professional duty.

Disrespectful communications between colleagues, between staff and parents and between workers and children and young people are destructive.

Reflection: things to discuss or think about

- In the example given above the message from the baby room worker to the mother – that she is superior and the mother is inferior – is not hidden, and might also be conveyed to any onlookers, including the children, as well as to the mother. Nevertheless the practitioner may be unaware of this and might protest 'I only told her that I'd shown her this morning… I didn't mean anything else by it.'

- Do you remember from your own experience any episodes where someone communicated, without saying it in so many words, that they were superior to someone else? What happened?

- Are there times in your work when you need to be especially careful not to communicate in this way?

- Which of the following pieces of advice would you give to a new member of staff (you are only allowed one): 'Try always to be tactful even if you don't feel like it' or 'Always show respect to people because they're fellow human beings with feelings just like you'?

OBSERVATION

- ☐ During the next few days be on the look-out for anyone trying to control another person – adult or child – by using blaming or moralising language. This could be in real life or on television. What happens?

Social inequality

Some communications contain harmful messages which convey the idea that certain groups of people are not valued to the same extent as others. The under-valued groups include people from minority ethnic communities, girls, gay and lesbian people and those who are mentally or physically disabled. Because they are under-valued, they are discriminated against and, as social groups, do not have equality with others – although individual members of these groups may nevertheless succeed and lead happy lives. Very early in life children come to understand the value that society at large places on different groups of people.

Sexism

Sexism is one example of social control, this time the ways in which women and girls are 'put in their place' by society at large and by institutions. It can operate in the way services are organised, how they are made available to the public and in their day-to-day practice. This is a wide area ranging from employment practice to language and behaviour which is insulting towards females.

Aspects of organisation may also carry messages. In classrooms, but even in less formal settings, girls may be asked to line up on one side of a room and boys on the other. Registers can be split between boys and girls, rather than being an alphabetic list of all the children attending. Boys and girls have been known to have separate games at a Christmas party. The staff organising the children on the basis of their sex may say that this is what they have always done, it 'doesn't mean anything' and it is just a way of organising the children. The hidden message to the children in these practices is that differences based on sex are very important. And so they are in biological rather than social contexts – unless we make them otherwise.

Homophobia

Some people are bullied because others perceive them as being a lesbian, gay, bisexual or transgender. The bullying can be physical, or can be through personal communication – which is the concern of this book. Verbal abuse, name-calling and imitation are forms of communication that are intended to hurt the other person and to claim superiority for oneself. As such they are in direct opposition to the values of social pedagogy which is based on equality and respect and the desire to support the confidence and self-esteem of all children.

Reflection: things to discuss and think about

What do you think are the controlling messages in these statements?

> TEACHER: Will one of the boys carry the chairs?

> CHILDMINDER: Big boys don't cry.

> PLAYWORKER: She's a real tom-boy!

> TEACHER: Girls on that side, boys over here.

> NURSERY OFFICER: We're going to ask if any of the fathers could help put up the stalls and if the mothers could make a cake.

> WARD SISTER: We put boys in blue cots, girls in pink.

> YOUNG PERSON: You're so gay! No, not really, it's only a joke.

Racism

Racism means all the ways in which people from minority ethnic groups are treated less favourably than other people in society and therefore put at a disadvantage. Racism has a long history, but it still exists today. Below we look at racist name-calling and so-called jokes as well as stereotyping messages. However, working against racism goes far beyond the interpersonal communications which are the subject of this book. Look out for the following indications of work which aims to be anti-racist.

In nursery work, play materials, books and toys have been chosen to which all the children and parents can relate. What about the pictures in books, on walls and in jigsaw pictures? Can all the children find people to identify with? If there are dolls, is their skin colour, hair and dress representative of the children using the service? Are there different paint colours available for different skin colours?

Does the home corner have a choice of foods and cooking utensils? Do staff know the names which children use for these? If they do not their communications with the children will be more difficult and may diminish children's self-esteem and pride in their ethnicity.

Even if there are no children from minority ethnic groups present, pictures and toys representative of the wider society are interesting for the other children. They also prepare them in a positive way for contact with people from other groups.

Some people may object that anti-racism practice is not important in their work, because they work with babies, and babies, they believe, are too young to be affected by these ways of working. However, learning about who you are and your social relationship with others starts at a very early age. At the heart of social pedagogy is the aim to do everything possible to support children and young people's confidence and self-esteem: they should grow up with a positive sense of their own identity.

Reflection: things to discuss or think about

'When I look at children I just don't see their colour. Children are children. I'm colour blind! I treat them all the same.'

- What would you say to a foster carer who said this?

Equality for children with disability

Disabled children provide an example of how children should not all be treated in the same way, in the name of equality. Some children have additional needs, which staff must meet in many different ways.

For example, of course there needs to be disability access, so that wheelchairs can get through doors and into toilets. There should also be positive images displayed – photographs and posters – showing people with disability taking an active part in events. There are many specialist books which tell the stories of children with different conditions: hearing impairment, spina bifida, and so on. All of these provide a focus for discussion between staff and children, giving children information and providing them with a language which they can use without embarrassment about the condition. As is the case with racism, expressions which are insulting to disabled people should always be challenged by staff (see Chapter 11).

Exercise: hidden messages

1. Hidden messages, about the value placed on different children, are to be found in the book corner. These messages depend on how representative the books are of the children present, and on the pictures within them. If the books are varied, and the pictures do not portray *stereotypical* (see p.115) images, story sessions can help communicate to the children that all are valued equally. But a skilled communicator and gifted story-teller would find it difficult to convey this message with books that were badly chosen.

   • Find a book or magazine that is popular with the people you work with. Go through it noticing the part, if any, played by females and males in the first five pictures.

   • Count how many men and boys there are compared with women and girls (if the book is about animals, very often it is clear if they are meant to be male or female).

- Is a girl or a woman, or a boy or a man in the foreground of the pictures? Is the person who is biggest a girl or a boy in each picture?

- Notice how often *male* characters are: taking the lead, active, watching someone else do something, helping someone else.

- How often are the *female* characters: taking the lead, active, watching someone else do something, helping someone else?

2. Are there any books available to children or young people about people from *minority ethnic groups*? What proportion is there?

  - In a book showing children from more than one ethnic group, repeat the exercise given in (1) above, but this time look at the different parts played by black people and white people.

3. Where you work, are there any books about disabled children *or young people*? What proportion is there?

  - Repeat the exercise given in (1) above, this time taking disabled children and young people as the subject. How usual is it to find a book containing positive images of children with disability?

When you've examined your book, decide if it contains any hidden messages about different social groups, for example: boys and girls, men and women, people from minority ethnic backgrounds. If other people have done this exercise, compare notes with them.

113

If children are limited to books with pictures like these then the suggestion is that girls and women provide an audience for boys and men, that boys are active, that black children are athletic, that the family car is for the men in the family while women are usually involved with child care, and that the normal family is white with two parents

Reflection: things to discuss or think about

1. You work in an inner-city school with children from different ethnic groups. It is Christmas and the teacher decides to put on a nativity play. She follows her usual practice: all the shepherds are played by boys, all the angels by girls; Mary is white, one of the three kings is black.

    *   Would you have any objections to the play?

    *   Why do you answer as you do?

2. You confront a young person about using a racist or sexist expression. She answers 'But my dad says that.' What sort of things could you say to her which would challenge what she had said yet also respect her relationship with her father?

3. What would you say to a child on a playscheme who was imitating a child with learning difficulties?

Name-calling

Very clear boundaries (see p.138) should be set precluding jokes and names that diminish whole social groups. This applies whether the expression used is written or spoken, used as a 'joke' or seriously, whether it is used by children who do not properly understand its meaning or when it is used by staff or by parents. Racist, sexist and homophobic language, and terms used to insult disabled people, hurt and demean. Although someone may excuse a young person or child, saying 'It's just a habit – he doesn't mean anything,' this is not the point. They are messages which are loaded with meaning about 'superiority' and the power that one social group has over another. They are also messages which help to maintain that power. So whether they are 'meant' or not, their use should always be challenged (see Chapter 11).

Stereotypes
Stereotyping leads to inequality

Hidden control messages are often contained in *stereotypes*. Stereotyping is when we do not see people as individuals, but are more concerned with them as members of a group – such as an age group, a profession, a racial group, whether they are men or women, boys or girls, gay and lesbian or straight, able-bodied or disabled. When people use stereotypes they focus on characteristics which they believe are true of all the members of that group. Stereotyping can include statements about supposedly good points as well as bad ones. Here are some examples of stereotyping that you may notice in work with children.

'Black children are naturally good at music'

Stereotypes can be about 'good' qualities as well as unpleasant ones. But if someone says 'Black people are all born singers and they've got a natural sense of rhythm' then he or she is denying them their essential individuality. Some black children are very musical, others are average, and others not very good. Stereotyping is a way of lumping people together, ignoring ways in which they are different.

'Boys are more adventurous than girls'

In fact some girls are more daring than some boys. Some boys are not daring at all. By the things they say and do workers can pass this attitude on to children, so that girls may not feel free to play with adventurous equipment. For example, at the Annual General Meeting of one playscheme, a report was accompanied by many slides showing boys swinging, climbing and being adventurous. The speaker made comments on the slides like 'They're real lads, aren't they?' The photographs could have shown girls using the swings (because they *did* use them) but instead the speaker had, unconsciously, been controlled by a common stereotype and was re-enforcing it for the audience. The indirect message was: 'This equipment is for boys.' The harm is done on two fronts: girls do not feel permitted to be adventurous and boys do not feel adequately 'male' if they prefer quieter pursuits.

'A mother's place is in the home'

This old-fashioned saying is one of the ways in which women have been 'kept in their place'. Both mothers and fathers have important roles to play at work *and* at home.

'People with learning difficulties do not experience grief in the way other people do'

When people are bereaved, no doubt there are many individual differences in how they experience this – whether they have learning difficulties or not. It is unrealistic and disrespectful to deny a child (or adult) the experience of grief on the grounds that they cannot understand. It is always better to acknowledge people's sadness; not to do so implies that they are not fully human.

'The people round here don't really care about their kids'

This stereotype writes off all the parents in a neighbourhood. It shows great disrespect and it must be inaccurate. Staff who use this sort of statement are claiming their own superiority and are probably out of touch with the lives and experience of the families using their service. Even if what they say seems to be true of certain individuals, staff should ask themselves what might be the reasons for a parent's apparent lack of care – for example if it is due to poverty, ill health or unemployment.

'Gay men are very sensitive'

Some are, some are not. As with any other stereotype, attributing certain characteristics to particular social groups is a way of pigeonholing them and stressing their 'otherness': they are different from people seen as 'normal'.

Stereotypes can interfere with communication

Like other controlling messages, stereotyping can be a powerful source of interference for the person affected by it, that is it can block or distort communication (see p.47). Anyone who is aware of being stereotyped often feels angry or humiliated and can become defensive, unprepared to listen. This is hardly surprising as the use of a stereotype shows that the speaker is highly aware of the other as a member of a particular group, with its supposed characteristics – good or bad. These characteristics may in themselves be offensive but, whether they are or not, the speaker shows that they do not see the other person as an individual. Also, the person who is being stereotyped is at risk of being dismissed as 'having a chip on their shoulder' and not listened to with respect.

Stereotypes also cause problems for those holding them, distorting how they experience other people, leading them to see and hear what they expect to see and hear, rather than what is actually happening. This is a dangerous practice when the result is to keep people in a position of inequality. Critically it may deny some children and young people access to a full range of resources intended for them to develop skills and learn new ones. When people hold stereotypes, they are likely to encourage characteristics which fit in with the stereotypes. This happens when they support boys in boisterous play and suggest quieter occupations for girls, for example. They may even excuse undesirable behaviour in the light of a fixed way of thinking about children: boys may be permitted a certain amount of 'rough' behaviour that would be frowned on in girls: both sexes are moulded into ways of behaving which do not, in the long run, serve their best interests; they become limited in what they think of as appropriate behaviour; boys may learn that they should not cry, appreciate beauty or express more sensitive emotions; girls may not be assertive, use technical equipment or play rough-and-tumble games. Young people from minority ethnic groups may feel valued for whatever is exotic about their culture, but not for more everyday aspects of their lives and experience.

This is the problem: stereotypes serve to control people and keep them 'in their place'. The people who use stereotypes may be quite unaware of this, with no idea that their communications contain hidden messages which exercise power and control.

Reflection: things to discuss or think about

- In your experience, is there much stereotyping to be found in work with children?

- Can you think of any other 'positive' or seemingly harmless stereotypes as well as those given above?

- Can you remember any times when you have been stereotyped? How did you feel? What did you want to do?

OBSERVATION

☐ During the coming week become aware of any stereotyping at work, on television or elsewhere.

Control and disrespect: key points

- Many interpersonal communications contain messages about control. Some of these are quite open as one person exercises, or tries to exercise, power over another by insulting them or moralising about their behaviour or putting them down in some other way.

- There are also less direct messages which result in and sustain social inequality between groups of people: men and women, different ethnic groups, disabled people, gay men and lesbians, young and old, rich and poor and others. These can include stereotyping and 'jokes' at the expense of these groups.

- Social pedagogues aim to treat all people with respect and to support children and young people's self-esteem and positive attitude towards their own identity. They expect that the other people with whom they share their living space, children or colleagues, will behave in the same way.

- Disrespectful communications between colleagues, between staff and parents and, most important of all, between workers and children are destructive and should be challenged (see Chapter 11).

- Disrespectful messages can be a source of interference in interpersonal communication because of the distracting emotions they arouse.

- Stereotypes can be a means of controlling people belonging to minority social groups by suggesting what behaviour is expected and acceptable from them. This is a way of 'keeping people in their place' and contributes to sexism, racism and other unjust systems.

- Treating people equally does not mean treating them all in exactly the same way.

CHAPTER 10

Conflict
When You are Criticised

Whatever your employment, situations are bound to arise when you are directly involved in conflict arising from your work, when the subject matter of your communication will centre on differences or disagreements between yourself and others. There will be times when another person, perhaps your manager, perhaps a parent or an angry child will be critical of something you have done and will tell you about it. On other occasions, you yourself may have concerns about someone's behaviour and decide, for professional reasons, to talk to them about it. In dealing with conflict you need to be aware of the three Ps: the professional, the personal and the private, because all three are relevant (see the Introduction to this book). As a professional you will want to obtain the best result for all concerned, especially the children and young people you work with. But personal feelings (including private ones) will also come into play.

People react differently to such situations depending on the circumstances, on who is involved and on their own particular temperament. But interpersonal conflict does not necessarily have negative results; it can be a starting point from which people come to understand one another better, take more account of the other's point of view and find constructive solutions to their differences. Occasions when differences are expressed honestly and listened to with respect can be very creative. For social pedagogues, this understanding informs all their work, whether with individuals or with groups.

This chapter shows you how to make use of what you have learned so far about interpersonal communication in what can be a particularly difficult circumstance: when you are at the receiving end of criticism. It aims to help you to work, as a professional, for a positive outcome when someone *confronts* you about something: when they openly tell you that in some way or other you are causing them a problem. The criticism may be delivered with some tact or, on the other hand, the other person may not consider your feelings at all and be, in your eyes, quite offensive – they may use the blaming and moralising approach discussed in the last chapter.

Nobody likes being criticised, even when the criticism is justified. It can shake your confidence and leave you feeling upset and angry, especially if the criticism is expressed with hostility and aggression. Nevertheless there are things you can do in the face of criticism which are constructive and which can help to build good relationships with colleagues and others.

There are five steps to be taken.

1. Keep cool: avoid making the situation worse

It is often easier to say 'keep cool' than to do it. However, keeping cool in the face of criticism may be absolutely necessary for the good of all concerned. If someone has reached the point where they feel that they must do something about a situation where they feel they must confront another person, feelings are probably already running high. These could complicate matters and make things worse. The person who has the problem and who decides to come out with it feels aggrieved, but in addition they may also feel anxious about voicing their complaint. The person at the receiving end of the complaint is also likely to feel their emotions rising. However, they have a responsibility to see that their feelings do not stand in the way of good professional practice. It is important to make sure that the situation does not go from bad to worse.

For example, a mother is angry with a childminder because she thinks her child has been playing in the garden, without being warmly dressed. The child has recently had a bad cold. She is nervous about approaching the minder and is feeling quite agitated. She summons up her courage and complains in a loud voice.

The minder's immediate reaction is of panic, followed by anger that the mother should speak to her so 'rudely'.

If the childminder allows her own feelings to become involved and shows them to the mother, the situation could escalate into

121

something far worse, into a row in fact, a situation containing so much interference (see p.47) that neither side would really hear what the other had to say. The childminder would not be open to the mother's very real anxieties about her child and the mother would not hear any explanation which the minder might offer.

If someone criticises you, justifiably or not, you need to be aware both of your own feelings and of those of the other person. It may be only too clear how the other person is feeling mainly through non-verbal signals: how they use their voice, their facial expression, and so on. They may look angry, raise their voice or gesticulate emphatically. When you are confronted by someone, whether an angry child or a senior colleague, who is showing strong, angry emotions, you need to be alert to signs of agitation or anger arising in yourself. If you ignore your feelings, you may communicate your agitation to the other person, causing the emotional temperature to rise still further. In such cases, a conscious effort to calm down is useful. Some people follow the old custom of literally counting up to ten, this at least stops them from saying the first thing which comes into their head. Or you could take some slow deep breaths. Just telling yourself to keep calm can also help, but you may need to remind yourself more than once.

A cooling-off period is going to be necessary before
these two can start to work things out

If the other person is very upset you should make a decision about whether your conversation should happen 'here and now'. Is a school gate, with other parents listening, a suitable place for talking to a visibly angry parent? If the cook in the residential home where you work is very upset about a decision which has affected her timetable, criticises you abusively in front of young people, what would be a constructive first step? To take another example, should you allow a noisy confrontation to take place in a baby room? Would a 'cooling-off period' help? Is there any way that you could postpone the conversation whether for five minutes or for a day or more, in order to take the heat out of the situation? If you do try to obtain a cooling-off period, or wish to move the conversation to a more suitable location be careful not to appear to be dismissive of the person or of their grievance. People have their own perspectives on how your actions, or those of your colleagues, affect them. Explain that you are taking the complaint seriously but that you could give it more careful consideration if you could talk about it in a quieter place or at a time when you could give it your full attention. Do not be vague about where and when you could meet to listen to what they have to say. Be specific about arranging a time and place which would suit both of you.

Exercise: suggesting a suitable time and place

Find as many ways as you can of saying, tactfully, that you would like to put off holding what looks like becoming a heated discussion until another time.

---

2. Listen, then let the other person know you understand

The importance of listening carefully to criticism must be emphasised. Let the other person have their say without interrupting: hear them out. It is important to try to understand other people's points of view. Then let them know that you understand the substance of their criticism by *reflecting back* what they have said (see Chapters 5 and 6 on reflecting back) and acknowledging their feelings. This is also a way of checking that you really *do* understand the criticism.

For example, a colleague says to you 'I'm really fed up with the way you always leave equipment out on a Wednesday afternoon so that I've got to put it away when I come in on a Thursday morning. It's not good enough. I've not got time to do your work as well as my own. Just because you leave early on Wednesdays doesn't mean you can't clear up. I can't clear up your things and get on with everything I've got to do at the same time. Anyhow you should get the young people to help you.'

In such a situation it would be easy to rush to a defence or an excuse, but this would not let your colleague know that you understand how your actions have affected him. A reply that lets your colleague know that you have received the message would be the most useful first step. Something like 'You've always got to clear up my stuff on Thursdays and you can't get on with your own work?' This reflects the content of the criticism: your colleague has to tidy up after you. Even if you say this, it is still possible that they will not realise, to begin with, that you have really heard them and may repeat some of their complaint: 'I've got enough to do on Thursdays, I can hardly manage as it is.' Reflect back again, including reflecting their feelings: 'Because I don't clear up last thing on Wednesday, you feel under pressure on Thursday mornings.'

Lee, a residential care worker, comes to Lucy and complains that she has taken a girl out shopping when there had been an agreement that the young people should be encouraged to settle down to do homework when they got in from school. He is particularly annoyed because he thought that this particular girl was beginning to make real progress, he had supported her with her school work, it hadn't always been easy, and now Lucy was undermining his work. At first Lucy is angry because Lee's manner is abrupt. But she keeps calm and listens to Lee and lets him know that she understands the problem and his feelings about it. Then she explains that she took the girl out to help her buy ingredients needed for a school cookery lesson, the next day.

Any solution, explanation or apology you want to give may not be properly heard until the person making the criticism knows that you can understand their point of view, that you are not avoiding it or denying it; in short you are taking their complaint – their experience – seriously. In facing criticism, as in all interpersonal work, respecting the other person's experience is paramount, although it is not always easy. Social pedagogy is about developing a state of mind which says that other people – colleagues, parents, young people and children – have their own experience and circumstances, a distinctive 'life world' (p.9), which is different from your own and which must be taken seriously.

3. Apologise

If you are in the wrong, apologise.

Imagine you are a foster carer who was not at home when a social worker called, although the visit had been agreed in advance. The social worker phones her to find out what had happened. The foster carer had forgotten about the appointment and when she hears the social worker's voice, suddenly remembers and feels flustered and on the defensive.

Everyone makes mistakes sometimes; it is part of everyday life. If you have misunderstood or forgotten something or not realised how your actions would affect another person, the most realistic and respectful way forward is to acknowledge that the other person has a cause for complaint. Say that you are sorry and, if appropriate, tell the other person any steps you are going to take to put things right.

In the example given on p.124, you might reply, 'I'm sorry about the equipment, I thought that you'd want to use it, but I should have checked. I'll pack it away in future.'

4. Put misunderstandings right

In some cases, all that is necessary is to put right any misunderstanding that underlies a criticism. So in the first example given above (p.121), where a mother is worried about her child who had had a cold, she might have misunderstood. Having listened carefully, the best thing for the minder to say would be something like: 'You thought Carol went out to play, with her bad cough? I can understand why you're annoyed. But in fact she didn't go out at all, I've kept an eye on her all day.'

5. Win/win situations

If the case cannot be resolved by a simple explanation or apology, then the most useful attitude in any conflict is that both sides should be satisfied if at all possible – you want the best outcome for everybody. So, first try to understand the other person's point of view and the reasonableness of it. Start from the position that people don't complain without a reason, they have their own perspective on life and work and this is different from your own. Reflect back to them how you think you have affected them and given cause for complaint. Then try to explain your own point of view (the next chapter goes into this in greater detail) and invite the other person to join you in finding a solution that suits both of you –- even if there has to be some give and take. If you try to win at the expense of the other person, by putting them down in some way or stealing an advantage, you may find that both of you (and therefore the others with whom you work) lose out.

For example, Steve, a nursery worker, comes to Nadina, in the next room, and complains that Nadina's group always has musical activities when his group is having a quiet time. Nadina feels quite flustered, but she listens to Steve and lets him know that she understands that her actions have caused difficulties for him.

Steve relaxes somewhat and Nadina explains that her group has music at that time because it's when it is their turn to have the nursery's musical instruments – but she's sorry for the disturbance. She asks Steve if they can think of any solutions between them. They think of all sorts of ways out of the problem including using different rooms and swapping round the times when different groups use the musical instruments. In the end they come up with an idea that suits both of them, to the benefit of both their groups.

Reflection: things to discuss or think about

- Can you remember times when having something out with someone – or their having it out with you – seemed to clear the air? Have there been other occasions when relationships have deteriorated after criticisms were made? Were there any differences in how matters were handled in these different cases?

- Which of the five ways of coping with criticism would you find most difficult? Cooling the situation down; listening and showing that you understand the other person; apologising or finding a win/win solution? Do different people find some of these aspects more difficult than others?

- If a child criticises a worker to their face, what should the worker do?

Exercise: receiving criticism

- If any incident arises in which you are criticised, at work or elsewhere, use the skills you have learned about in the session.

- Later write notes about it – what happened, how you responded and the outcome.

- What was difficult? Were there any surprises?

ROLE PLAYS

- Reg is the father of Gary, aged two. He found bite marks on Gary's leg yesterday evening and is very upset. He speaks to Sally, Gary's nursery worker, about it first thing the next morning.

  Try the role play twice; once with Sally being on the defensive and then with her trying to be as constructive as possible, in the ways that have been suggested in this chapter.

- Lela, who works in a children's residential home, has planned a special meal. The young people have chosen the menu and will cook it themselves and decorate the table. Lela has been out, buying some last-minute ingredients. When she gets back the young people tell her that Samuel, another worker, has put some chicken pieces and chips in the oven and told the young people to go and watch television; he would call them when the meal was ready. The young people crowd round to hear what Lela will say to Samuel. She is feeling quite angry.

Again try the role play twice, once with Samuel being on the defensive and a second time when he tries to be as constructive as possible, in the ways suggested above.

Receiving criticism: key points

If you find yourself at the receiving end of criticism or complaints at work, the following points can help you to be constructive, to the advantage of everyone concerned, particularly the children or young people with whom you work:

- Remember the three Ps of social pedagogy (the professional, the personal and the private). Be professional – use all your skills to serve the best interests of the children and respect your colleagues – but also be aware of your own personal feelings and how these can affect your response in ways that are not constructive.

- If necessary, cool the situation down. Be aware of any interference caused by your own personal feelings and do what you can to keep calm. Notice the non-verbal communication of feelings coming from the other person.

- Try to see the other person's point of view and let them know that you understand. Reflect back what they say to you. This helps to clarify their complaint and is one way of showing that you respect them.

- Everyone makes mistakes sometimes, so apologise if you are in the wrong.

- If there is a misunderstanding, clear it up by explaining what has actually happened.

- Avoid a win/lose situation and use all your interpersonal skills to see that you both 'win'. Suggest that both of you think of all the different ways you can to get round the difficulty and together choose the one which is most mutually satisfactory.

CHAPTER 11

Conflict

Confronting Problems

The last chapter was about times when someone had a complaint and you found yourself at the receiving end of criticism. This chapter looks at the other side of the coin. In society we do not all share the same perspectives and we can have many different reasons for acting as we do. This chapter is about situations when you feel the need to *confront* another person – adult, child or young person – about their actions. You decide that you should tell them directly about whatever is troubling you, in order to solve a problem. Again, social pedagogues would say that working with conflict, not denying it, is a creative process.

For people at the beginning of their careers, including students, it is often – not always – better to consult a senior worker, rather than approaching the person directly concerned. It would always be better to get advice if the matter was serious or if you were worried about what to do. The service you are working in may have a policy about the use of racist or sexist language and bullying, about young people swearing, or about parents being late collecting children. You need to find out about this if you do not already know. Also it may be that senior workers have information about a child or their family which needs to be taken into account. They may, therefore, decide that it is they who should take any action rather than leave it to someone who is still inexperienced.

A decision to confront someone about a problem arising from their behaviour should only be taken for good, professional reasons. A professional reason would be that the other person's actions are not in the best interest of the children. Or it might be that their behaviour has adverse consequences for you or your work. For example:

- In an under-fives playgroup there is a mother who does not get involved with the children or help in any way, but sits on the side all the time.

- At a picnic for foster carers and their families, a support worker finds a quiet corner to smoke a cigarette, but is still in full view of the children.

- A colleague in a young people's residential home does something that seems thoughtless. Perhaps they chat for a long time on the phone before they go off shift, leaving little time to explain to you when you arrive for your shift, how the day has gone so far. There had been some problems on the previous day, so you feel rather insecure about how the young people will behave. You will have to ask another member of staff about things, but it will be difficult to find a quiet moment to do so.

- You are a childminder. A parent is frequently late picking up his child. You believe that the child becomes anxious when his father does not turn up on time. In addition the father is breaking his agreement to collect his child punctually. This has an effect on your feelings – you feel resentful – and you cannot leave the house until he turns up.

- One child is aggressive towards another and uses racist insults towards him. You think that this is undesirable for both children.

In all of these cases you have a choice: either to put up with what is troubling you or to do something about it by confronting the person involved.

Although keeping quiet about a problem has its attractions, and no doubt you can think of cases where allowing a cooling-off time (see Chapter 10) is clearly the best course, there are also occasions when to do nothing is a mistake, and you must take action. For example staff working with children cannot stand by and allow them to hurt one another. But circumstances may not always seem so urgent and staff can put off confronting someone about a problem, even when they know it is necessary. This may be because they are afraid that the other person will react in an angry fashion. Or it may be because they feel over-protective and fear that challenging someone about their behaviour would be damaging to them in some way. Whatever the reason practioners can bottle up their feelings with the result that their resentment is shown in other, less direct ways. Eventually, when they can put up with the situation no longer, they explode with anger and more damage is done than if the problem had been tackled earlier. The person under attack justifiably feels aggrieved and may say words to the effect of 'Why didn't you tell me before? I didn't know I was causing problems.'

Clearly it is better to confront 'unacceptable behaviour' earlier rather than later, so that it does not develop into an even larger problem. Do not behave as though someone else can read your mind; they need to be told if they are causing you concern. It is reassuring to realise that confrontation can be handled well — so that no one is unduly hurt and there is a satisfactory outcome. Ways of doing this will be given in this chapter.

But staff need also to think whether problems arise because of the way in which a service is organised. Social pedagogues are encouraged to consider how both the wider society and the service in which they work can contribute to difficulties. For example, there may be only one of a particularly popular piece of play equipment and this seems to be at the root of some aggressive behaviour between children. This is a problem which staff must work to solve, asking themselves questions such as: how can we help the children to share things with one another, generally, not just with this piece of equipment? Do we need more than one of these toys? Is there a fair way of organising turns which everyone can agree about? Should we ask the children to put their minds to this as a group? Bringing children and young people into problem-solving respects them as members of society, social participants, and shows that staff value their contributions.

Reflection: things to discuss or think about

- Can you think of any situation which has deteriorated because someone has put off confronting another person about their behaviour?

- In your experience are there occasions when it is better not to confront another person about behaviour which is causing you problems?

- Do staff always agree as to what is 'acceptable' or not? Can you think of examples? What problems can arise from this and what should be done about it?

How to confront constructively

Remember that you are confronting the other person about a problem which arises as a result of their behaviour. *You are not criticising them as a person.* Your aim is that the difficulty is overcome, without damage to your relationship and the other person's self-esteem. This is always important and it is crucial in work with children and young people.

Stay calm

Do not challenge someone about their behaviour when you are feeling very agitated. Just as when you are yourself on the receiving end of criticism, you need to be sufficiently in control to be constructive and to chose your words carefully. If your feelings are not under control you may say things which undermine relationships and which you will regret later. Remember a display of anger or annoyance can arouse feelings in the other person which interfere with how they receive your 'message'. There is a strong possibility that they will not really listen, but be taken up with their own feelings of anger, anxiety or shame resulting from what they see as an unexpected 'attack'. So remind yourself to stay calm.

Choose the right time and place

You have to decide when is the right time and place for confronting someone about their behaviour. For example, in the heat of the moment, when you are feeling angry or hurt about something, you may not be able to confront a problem in such a way that there is a good outcome. If a young person switches television stations while others are watching and shouts angrily when they protest, it may be better to wait for them to calm down before you take any further action. Similarly, a moment when an adult is obviously distressed about something may not be a good time to bring up a problem.

Check misunderstandings

Once you have decided to confront someone, the first step is to check, politely and sincerely, that there is no misunderstanding, on your part or that of the other person, which is causing the problem. This gives you the opportunity to back down gracefully if the mistake is on your part, and the other person the chance to apologise if the mistake is theirs.

Sometimes this is enough. For example:

> TEACHING ASSISTANT: Excuse me, did you know I'd just cut all that paper to take for Rainbow Room?

> TEACHER: Oh, I'm sorry, I thought it was for us.

Or you could check whether you understand the situation properly:

> PLAYWORKER: Why did you throw all the dolls right across the room?

> CHILD: Because there was a fire and they all ran away.

And:

> PRACTIONER: Have I got it right, I thought you said Mary was going to help me on Fridays, but she thinks she should be in Sunshine Room?

> MANAGER: I'm so sorry, I forgot to tell her.

Or:

> MANAGER: No, if you remember that was for after Easter, when the new assistant comes.

In checking misunderstandings your non-verbal communication must back up the verbal communication. An accusing tone of voice could make the same words carry a very different meaning. Imagine the effect of 'Excuse me, did you know I'd just cut all that paper to take for Rainbow Room?' snarled between clenched teeth!

All confrontation needs tact and sensitive handling but some situations call for special care. Such a case is the example (p.130) of the mother who does not get at all involved with the activities but always sits and watches. You should check if she understands what she should be doing at the playgroup – it could be that she thinks she is there only to keep an eye on the children. The discussion would need some introduction, perhaps about whether she enjoys being at the playgroup or if there are any difficulties. Possibly she feels shy and you need to help her find her feet by encouraging her, rather than by confrontation.

Before continuing with Steps 4 and 5, you might like to try the following exercise.

Exercise: when you want to challenge someone's behaviour

You could do this exercise individually, in pairs or as a whole group. In each of the examples below imagine that you are the person who is speaking, confronting the other about a problem. Find other, more effective ways of challenging the other person. Suggest what you could say to open the conversation, checking if there is any misunderstanding on the part of the other person, or any difficulty that you do not know about.

- Ward sister to nursery nurse who is late for the fourth time in succession: 'You're very unpunctual!'

- Senior playworker to a student who is chatting in the staff room about some sensitive personal details disclosed to her by a child's mother: 'You're not supposed to gossip like that. It's not professional.'

- Residential worker to a colleague who has opened a letter addressed to her: 'How dare you! You've been reading my private correspondence!'

- Playworker to caretaker: 'Why is the floor in the hall wet? Why didn't you clean it earlier like you're supposed to? It's really dangerous, the children were slipping all over it...'

- Foster carer to teenager: 'I've never met such an untidy child. Haven't you been taught to clear up after yourself?'

- Childminder to mother who comes late to pick up the children: 'It's really inconsiderate, coming late like this.'

- After-school worker to five-year-old who did not hang up her coat: 'You're such a lazy girl today.'

Do not blame

If the other person does not understand your problem, you need to help them to see things from your point of view. It will be difficult to achieve their co-operation, however, if you antagonise them. So, in telling them about the problem do not blame them or moralise about their behaviour, or comment on their character. Doing so disrespects the other person. It also causes interference (see p.47) which stops people from listening and hinders them from seeing your point of view.

With the foster carer, in the above example, perhaps the strongest message that the teenager gets is that the carer does not approve of him. Avoiding blaming people is vital, but it may not come naturally. Many of us are accustomed to situations where blame and criticism are used in order to control – or attempt to control – others (see pp.105–7). Blaming does not give clear information about the behaviour that is causing a problem – because it focuses on the person and not on the behaviour. The message that it sends is that the other person – child or adult – is not of value, not worthy of respect. As such it can lower their self-esteem and damage the trust between you.

Reflection: things to discuss or think about

Perhaps you can remember times when you have been at the receiving end of criticism and how you felt about it. In the example below, see how many examples you can spot of moralising and blaming. What effect are Jean's communications having on Yusef?

Jean, the nursery's deputy manager, is just about coping today. The manager is on leave and two people who work in the baby room have phoned in to say that they are sick, leaving only Yusef, a newly appointed member of staff to be on duty there. Jean herself is the only other person on the staff with experience of looking after babies so she decides to cover the baby room herself.

She is called to the phone about an emergency admission. Before she goes, she asks Yusef to wash the bottle just used by the youngest baby and to bring the play pen and toys back in from the garden – it looks as though it's going to rain.

Jean is away longer than she had hoped. She returns to find that Yusef has not washed the bottle nor brought the things in from the garden. As she thought, the rain is starting to fall. Dinner for the older babies will soon arrive from the kitchen, but nothing is ready. Yusef is sitting with one baby on his knee and one crawling on the mat in front of him. The others are in their cots. The following conversation takes place:

JEAN: Look, Yusef, you've not done anything I asked you to. I expected you to get on so we'd be ready for the dinners when I got back. Instead I find you sitting there playing with the babies. You're just not pulling your weight.

YUSEF: I thought... I mean I couldn't do everything and Donna was crying and I thought I was supposed to...

JEAN: I asked you to do something and you just took no notice. You haven't even washed the bottle out. It's not good enough, you're supposed to be a trained nursery worker – I'd have been better off with a first-year student.

YUSEF: (*sulkily*) I couldn't find the bottle brush and Donna started to cry so I picked her up...

JEAN: Look, here's the bottle brush, under your nose. Now for goodness sake get on with it and try to get things ready by the time I come back.

'I' language and 'you' language

Blame and criticism are often used to persuade people to change their behaviour, but they should be avoided. Instead, if you need to confront another person, tell them how their actions affect you and your work, including your professional responsibilities towards parents and children. If appropriate, explain how other people are affected by the behaviour in question.

Say what the matter is from your point of view: 'I feel... I need... I have a problem.' This is known as using 'I' language. The emphasis is on 'me', my responsibilities and needs, and the problems that arise for 'me', whether personally or professionally, as a result of the other person's actions. 'You' language, on the other hand, puts the emphasis on criticising and blaming the other person. 'You' language tells someone that they are awful, inconsiderate, untidy, and produces interference and hostility.

A useful formula for talking about how the other person's actions affect you is: 'When you...I feel...' For example:

'When you were on the phone so long this morning, I felt really rushed and worried that I was not going to get everything done.'

Not:

'It's really inconsiderate leaving me to do all the work, while you waste time chatting to your friends on the phone.'

The first approach gives the other person information they might not have had before: that their actions put pressure on you. This in itself may be enough to bring about a change in their behaviour. It could also be an opportunity for them to tell you any good reason for the long phone call. This positive way of dealing with problems clears the air and makes for good working relationships.

Setting boundaries

The word 'social' in social pedagogy refers to the fact that we live our lives with other people, in society. One result is that in different ways, we agree about what is desirable behaviour and what is unacceptable. There are boundaries, in society at large, in our homes and where we work that mark a line between what is acceptable and what is not. They are not necessarily set top-down, but are generally understood by the people involved.

Boundary-setting: children

You sometimes need to let children know about boundaries, about what is acceptable and what is not. With a baby or toddler a firm 'No', accompanied by removing them from the situation lets them know that you do not accept certain behaviour – when a baby pulls another child's hair, for example. With older children and young people, telling them about what is acceptable should be accompanied by the reasons why. Giving reasons can appeal to their own sense of fairness and shows that you take them seriously – they are not there just to obey orders without explanation.

If one child hits another, you separate them and say to the aggressor: 'We don't hit other people – it hurts.' In this way you protect one child and give the other a clear understanding of what is expected. This makes for security; children know where they stand. You are also giving a reason for the rule, which helps the child realise that other people have feelings and rights, too – you are helping to bring children up as social beings, not merely as individuals.

In Chapter 9 there were several examples of unacceptable behaviour that hurts others because it insults their ethnic identity, sex, sexuality or disability. The examples included so-called jokes and name-calling. Children and young people should be told that these words and ways of speaking about people are not acceptable because they are hurtful; a clear boundary needs to be set.

Sometimes what a child does is against their own best interests, rather than harming someone else. For example, a child or young person may do something which is dangerous: they may persist in using craft equipment in a dangerous way, contrary to your instructions. Say something like: 'Hold the knife by the handle,' demonstrate how this should be done and see that he or she complies with your instruction. Or you might find a 12-year-old drinking a can of beer. Again, because children sometimes need to be protected from the results of their own behaviour, the boundaries should be made clear: tell them that drinking alcohol is not allowed and give reasons.

It may also be necessary to ask a child for explanations for unacceptable behaviour to clear up any misunderstandings and to provide more information about the child's point of view. It may be better to use a non-threatening question such as 'What happened?' rather than 'Why did you do that?'

Children and young people can set their own boundaries as a group, about what is acceptable and what is not. They can make rules that can be referred to in order to settle disputes, because everyone has agreed. An example is that young people agree that they should sign up for table tennis and snooker to make sure that everyone has a turn.

All of the above suggests that boundary-setting should be accompanied with explanation and an appeal to children's sense of fairness. However this approach is not always taken and it has been known for staff to take more punitive measures such as shouting at young people, making children sit in the corner or even handling them roughly. These are powerful communications, messages conveying that 'might is right'. They ignore children's own developing sense of justice and their growing ability to reason. They can also damage their self-esteem, rather than build it up, which is an important aim of social pedagogy.

Reflection: things to discuss or think about

- 'I think you should tell children off if they do something wrong like hurt someone else or take their things. You should tell them that they're naughty.' What do you think of this opinion?

- Is there any difference between a member of staff telling a child off and a mother doing it?

Boundary-setting: adults

Here is an example of a confrontation with an adult which involves setting boundaries.

You are in charge of a children's centre. A mother smokes in the garden while she is with her children. Clearly it is your responsibility to see that this does not happen and so you must speak to her about it. In the first place you should check that she knows about the rule and make the boundaries clear: 'Did you know we've got a no-smoking rule, including in the garden, when the children are here?' This gives her information which she might not already have; it also gives her the chance to back down gracefully. If she persists you need to tell her where you stand and what your responsibilities are, using 'I' language: 'I have to see that the no-smoking policy is carried out,' 'We don't smoke in front of children because it sets a bad example' and 'I'm concerned for the children's health.'

It is important to show that you understand her point of view and the effects this rule is going to have for her, for example that you are sorry for any consequences of your action: 'I'm sorry you're missing your cigarette.' But it's not helpful to apologise for asking her to keep to the rules – setting and maintaining boundaries is part of your job. So saying 'I'm sorry I've got to ask you to stop smoking' is just not appropriate, in fact it may not even be sincere.

Reflections: things to discuss or think about

- What is the difference between saying that you are sorry for any consequence of asking a person to keep to the rules, and saying you are sorry about imposing a rule?
- Could you make up some more examples of these, based on your own work?

Think of solutions: problem-solve

As we saw earlier when there is conflict it helps to be creative, to find ways out that satisfy both sides – 'win/win' solutions (see p.126) – and involve the other person in finding them. Invite them directly to think of ways round the problem: 'You want to smoke but I am not allowed to permit smoking here. Can we come up with a way out?'

In the example above the mother could go to a nearby pavement cafe while you played with the children (although you wish she did not smoke at all). But, again, there could be difficulties with this solution. Would the children be happy? Do you have conflicting duties that mean you have not got time to give the children proper attention? In the course of problem-solving people may need to suggest several ideas before you find something mutually acceptable.

Problem-solving with children

It is also possible to use problem-solving with children once they are old enough to understand the approach. If a child is going against the interests of other people point out that this behaviour is not permitted: that is, set the boundaries (see p.138), and briefly give the reason, for example, 'We don't hit other people, because it hurts them.' Then ask for the child's reason for what occurred:

'What happened?'

'She's got my car and I want it.'

Next involve the child in suggesting other ways of obtaining the required result: 'What else could you have done to get your car back?' Children soon get used to this approach and come up with ideas for themselves. You are helping them to be creative and to realise that they have choices about their own behaviour. They also learn that there are socially acceptable ways of solving their own problems.

ROLE PLAY

- You may be able to think of times when you wanted to confront a problem but were nervous of speaking to the person concerned. Choose one such occasion for a role play. Do it twice, the first time ignoring the advice given in this chapter. The second time, handle the confrontation as constructively as possible.

- How did it feel, each time, from your point of view and from that of the other person?

- What did the onlookers notice?

Exercise: confronting problems

Here is an opportunity to practise confronting problems so that you can do it effectively should the occasion arise. Choose a partner and each take a turn with both parts in the small scenarios suggested below. After each example talk about how you both felt – was it a successful communication from your point of view? What further possibilities can you think of about approaching the other person and solving the problem?

1. The manager of a young people's residential home speaks to a member of staff who is late when coming on duty for the third time in a month.

2. A nursery worker confronts a mother who continually forgets to bring back clothing – pants and tights – lent when the child wet herself at nursery. The nursery is running out of spares.

3. A playworker speaks to a colleague about always taking too long a coffee break.

OBSERVATION

☐ During the next week or so be aware of instances involving conflicts as they occur around you – for example at work, in a shop or on television. Include confrontations between adults and between adults and children.

☐ How do both parties react? Are the confrontations handled well is there a creative outcome?

☐ Check what happens against the key points given below, and decide what has the most effect on the outcome. If you are involved in conflict at work, is the outcome what you hoped to achieve? Is it effective in terms of your professional aims and values?

Confronting problems: key points

- Sometimes it is professionally necessary to speak to other people, adults and children, about any difficulties their behaviour is causing. If they are doing things which work against children's best interests, either directly or otherwise, then you should speak to them about it and find a way forward together.

- Living together in society is bound to result in conflicts. These should be addressed creatively and in accordance with your professional aims and values.

- Challenge the problem, not the person. Do not blame, moralise or tell off.

- Do not confront people of whatever age in ways that may lower their self-esteem and confidence.

- When you confront a problem, stay calm in order to avoid interference (see p.47).

- Use 'I' language, explaining how you and other people are affected by the other's actions.

- Try to find 'win/win' solutions to conflicts. Addressing conflicts constructively can be a creative process, the basis for good relationships and healthy social life.

CHAPTER 12

Communicating in Groups and Meetings

People who work with children and young people sooner or later have to take part in meetings and other forms of face-to-face communication in groups. Being in a group of some sort is a familiar experience for everyone. From childhood we have all belonged to many different groups. We start off in a particular type of group, the family, with parents or carers and perhaps brothers and sisters and other relatives. Then our social world expands. At an early age many of us go to nurseries and playgroups where we start to learn about being members of a wider society that goes beyond our families. We all went to school, where we were members of class and peer groups. In our free time we may have attended play services and taken part in varied group activities or we may have participated in Scouts, Guides or youth groups. In adult life we experience working with a group of colleagues and may also be members of formal and informal groups in our leisure time. Social pedagogy is especially interested in the social aspects of our lives. Much of the work of social pedagogues aims at supporting people to make a positive contribution to society as members of the various educational, leisure or working groups to which they belong.

The subject of this chapter is a certain sort of group: face-to-face meetings in which you participate professionally, whose aim is to create co-operation and communication. These groups may involve children, young people, parents and/or staff. Some meet only once, others meet frequently on a regular basis. They are often brought together to draw on the experience, energy and skills of many people, whether the group meets once or is ongoing. In social pedagogy, the value of reflecting together in groups is recognised. However, reflection is not seen as mere discussion and exchange of thoughts. We said earlier that social pedagogues think of themselves as 'head, hands and heart'. That is, as professionals they are thoughtful practitioners (the head) at the same time they are practical and value action (the hands) and recognise that they have feelings about their work (the heart). Head, hands and heart all have a part to play when people come together as a group.

A regular meeting in a residential home gives young people the opportunity to be heard on issues that concern them as a group, whether these are plans for activities and outings, or any difficulties that are arising. In other services, parents and staff sometimes meet together to talk about mutual interests and concerns. Regular staff meetings are also usually held to plan and review projects, to confront difficulties, and to exchange ideas and necessary information.

A group meeting is a means of bringing out the best in people when it encourages its members to be creative in ways that would have not occurred to them as individuals. Groups also give their members an opportunity to experience, at first hand, that there may be many perspectives on life and work, as well as their own. But meetings do not always function well. If they are managed badly or if people do not take a proper responsibility for playing their part as best they can, groups can be boring, frustrating and even destructive. People who have had unsatisfactory experience in groups may feel very reluctant to attend or be responsible for what they see as 'yet another meeting'.

Groups need careful attention if they are to get off to a good start and they need commitment to keep them functioning well. What follows is some practical information about group work. There is advice on how to make your own best contribution as a group member. The chapter also covers bringing together and leading different sorts of groups, so that they fulfil their potential by drawing on the talents and experience which different members have to offer.

Types of group

There are different sorts of groups for different tasks, and different types of group leadership. Broadly speaking these types may be reduced to three: directed groups; facilitated groups for sharing experience or mutual support; and collaborative groups.

A directed group

A directed group is not the main subject of this chapter, but it is included because it provides a useful contrast with the two types of group described later.

A highly experienced person may call on a group of other people to work under his or her direction. For example, in a crisis a person with particular skills and knowledge may direct others. If there is a traffic accident, involving several people, a qualified first aider may take charge and tell others what to do – asking someone to phone for medical and police help, saying who may be moved, asking someone to find coats to cover anyone in shock, looking after those who need urgent attention. She or he explains what is to be done and how to do it, checks that instructions have been carried out, and puts right mistakes. The others accept this type of leadership because they recognise that expertise is necessary if lives are to be saved and no time wasted. They may be highly creative people, full of ideas, but they are ready to put these to one side in these circumstances.

The same sort of directive leadership may be acceptable in other, less extreme, situations – when a group of volunteers comes together to refurbish a community centre under the direction of a professional painter and decorator, for example. The volunteers recognise the leader's expertise and get on with the job as instructed. Of course they prefer it if the leader explains clearly, is good humoured, makes some allowance for their mistakes and is open to their suggestions.

Difficulties arise when someone adopts a directive leadership style when this is not absolutely necessary. If they do so, a group loses out on the rich contributions that its members can make, and the discoveries that come about when people are in 'dialogue', that is listening and learning from each other, finding ways of doing things and solutions to problems which, as individuals, would not have occurred to any of them.

Reflection: things to discuss or think about

- Have you had any experience of belonging to a directed group, such as those described above?
- How did you feel about it?

- What, if any, were the advantages and disadvantages?
- Have you ever felt that this type of leadership was used in circumstances where it was inappropriate?

A facilitated group for sharing experience or mutual support

The work of a group leader is not necessarily to instruct, supervise or organise. This sort of leadership would be inappropriate for a group where people come together for mutual support or to share their experience; for example:

- a group of parents who meet regularly to talk about bringing up children or teenagers
- colleagues who meet to support each other.

In groups like these, an effective leader sets out to provide the conditions in which members may feel at ease so that they are able both to make a contribution and to be attentive to other people. In such a group the leader is a facilitator, facilitating the group process but not directing the group members. Facilitators are not necessarily expert in the subject matter which is raised. They may facilitate a parents' group or a staff group, without themselves being parents or children's practitioners, or knowing at first hand the problems which members discuss. In this sort of group, the member's task is to share experience and support each other: the facilitator's is to see that this can happen.

If group members are not accustomed to a facilitated group, and are more used to being directed by an expert (as in the groups just described) they may feel confused at the way the facilitator treats the group and would like them to provide 'right answers', or to side with one group member as being 'correct' compared with another.

There is nothing wrong in setting out to give information and there is often a place for straightforward teaching. Staff may welcome a talk about something with which they are unfamiliar: play services, fostering or child care in other countries, for example. Or parents could ask for a meeting at which an expert talks about adolescent development. But these are not tasks for the facilitator of a group which comes together for mutual support. In support groups, there is the opportunity to speak about one's own experience and to listen to other group members; it is the facilitator's responsibility to see that it can happen. It is also important that new members understand that this is the nature of the group they are joining, otherwise they may become frustrated and angry, demanding to be given answers to the difficulties.

The 'collaborative group'

Quite a different sort of group from the above is a working group which has to make decisions or carry out a task. Individuals are invited to join such a group because they have some particular experience or skill to offer. Such groups collaborate, or work together, on some task. For example:

- A management committee engaged in recruiting new staff and making decisions about the person specification, the level of pay, advertising the vacancy, how to short-list candidates and who is to be involved in interviewing.

- An informal working party, composed of staff and parents, deciding how to let local people know about their summer festival: whether by leaflet, informing schools, putting up posters or whatever. They would also decide who was going to do what, if any others needed to be included in producing publicity material, and whether and when to hold further meetings.

In these cases, the group leader would have the role of chairperson. Just as with the facilitator (above) the person who chairs a collaborative group has the job of making sure that the best contribution can be made by every group member. There is no point in having expertise within the group if it cannot come to the surface and be of use. Some group members are very knowledgeable and can be turned to for information; others may have artistic or organisational talents; still others see ways of reconciling different points of view and suggesting ways forward if a group gets stuck. In a collaborative group, decisions are made about tasks. The chairperson has to keep the various tasks in mind, be ready to remind the group about them and move them forward when necessary. It is also the chairperson's work to see that all decisions and their outcomes are reviewed at the next meeting.

As you can see, in different sorts of groups the members and the leaders have different functions. Directive leaders act as experts and organisers, with all the knowledge and skills needed for a task. They know what needs to be done and how to do it. They just need a work team to carry out their directions. They see that work is carried out properly and that group members act as instructed. In support groups, facilitators concentrate their attention on the group, its members and their experience. In these groups there are no decisions to be made about work, or about any outside goals; the members' contributions are valuable in themselves.

In collaborative working groups the joint attention of the chairperson and of group members is, or should be, on the task in hand. Together they want to reach a certain goal, using all the expertise which is in the group and the creativity that can be such a rewarding part of working in a group.

Staff meetings

Sometimes different types of groups overlap. An example of this is staff meetings, which have characteristics of both supportive and collaborative groups. People have the opportunity to reflect on experiences and to support each other. At the same time, staff meetings are used to come to decisions and to exchange information. Staff need to be sensitive to these different processes and to act accordingly, being responsive and supportive listeners, aware of their own feelings and perspectives, but also recognising the group's need to address tasks in a business-like way. All members of staff should take responsibility for how well a meeting functions and if it meets their professional aims and values.

Responsibility for yourself

You are responsible for your contribution to the groups of which you are a member. You may find speaking up in a group easy or difficult; individuals are different – and that includes how they behave in groups.

Some people find it helpful to compare group members to different sorts of animals, to show the variety that is to be met. Some people are like nervous gazelles who allow other people to glimpse them, briefly, before darting swiftly away. Others are like the tortoise who slowly and certainly makes progress. Still others are like playful puppies: they jump right in, making quite a lot of noise, and enjoy themselves enormously. Others are like the owl, who stays silent for long periods, before swooping down on its prey.

Making an effective contribution

Here are some points which can help you to make an effective contribution, whatever creature you might resemble:

- If you have something to say, say it. This means being persistent and making sure that you are noticed by the rest of the group. Speak up clearly, as soon as another person stops speaking. In a more formal group, signal to the chairperson that you wish to speak next by raising your hand.

- Say what you have to say as plainly as possible and use concrete examples. Avoid jargon and unnecessary theory, they do not help people to understand what you mean.

- Be aware of your own feelings – are you feeling elated, anxious, sad, angry, bored? These feelings could affect how you contribute to the group. Being aware will help you to express yourself without your feelings getting in the way.

- Be willing to talk about your feelings, as well as about your ideas. Say 'I feel depressed when parents don't come to our evening meetings,' rather than 'The trouble is that in this society people are apathetic.'

- Do not hog the meeting by talking too much; be aware that others have a contribution to make and that the group will benefit from hearing all of its members.

Responding to other people

As well as taking responsibility for what you say, you need also to be sensitive towards other group members. The first part of this book describes how to listen in an encouraging way, being aware of other people's feelings and responding to them, and asking questions. In later chapters it describes how to play a positive part when conflict arises. The same approaches are often useful in groups as well as in encounters between individuals. It is the responsibility of group members to encourage one another to speak and to affirm one another's contributions. It is not just the business of the group leader. Especially important is to address other group members, not just the group leader (except, that is, in a very formal chaired meeting). This can get ideas flowing between group members. It also helps the flow of the meeting if you refer to what others have said when you take your turn to speak. In doing so you build on other people's contributions.

Here are some points which may help you in responding to other people:

- Be aware of other people's feelings. In formal meetings, these are often conveyed in non-verbal behaviour, more than what people actually say (see Chapter 1).

- Be prepared to confront other individuals about their behaviour, or the group as a whole if you think that this is appropriate (Chapters 10 and 11).

- Accept other people's talents, their experience and their willingness to take the lead during a meeting. Be happy at the richness that is available and the potential it provides for an effective group.

Be sensitive to the group

Just as individuals are different, so are groups. Some groups are warm and trusting, others seem to be rather cool, with individuals not communicating easily. There are groups which work enthusiastically; others find ways of avoiding whatever they set out to do, whether it is mutual support or fund-raising.

Here are some of the ways groups avoid getting on with whatever they have met to do:

- They spend a lot of time analysing and talking round the subject, without getting down to practical matters. For example a planning group might talk at length about local politics, but not choose someone to book premises so that a fund-raising event can take place.

- Some groups get side-tracked onto subjects which are not to the point and waste a lot of time.

- People generalise, they refuse to be specific. For example they do not talk about their own experience but say things like: 'Young workers are very unsure about how they should treat the children' rather than 'I didn't feel at all confident when I started work here' or: 'In the inner city people are often isolated' rather than 'Some of the mothers have told me they feel quite lonely and find it hard to make friends in the neighbourhood.'

- Others treat subjects flippantly or make jokes when it is not appropriate. This may discourage group members who are afraid of not being taken seriously.

- A group may allow one or two people to talk about their problems most of the time. This ignores the needs of other members, the contributions they could make and the work that is to be done.

- Some groups spend their time arguing.

- Some groups like to find scapegoats for their own failures. They blame outside circumstances or a particular group member for what goes wrong, rather than take group responsibility for any lack of progress.

If any of the above happens, the group is wasting its time and avoiding its main task. It is the responsibility of any member who notices this to confront the group about it (see pp.129–38). It is not the responsibility of the leader alone.

Reflection: things to discuss or think about

- Think about how you behave in meetings. What sort of creature would you compare yourself with?

- Have you experienced a successful group – one which fulfilled its purpose? What sort of contributions from group members helped this?

- Have you ever been in an unsuccessful group – one which did not fulfil its purpose? Can you identify any of the ways in which it avoided its task? Were they similar to those listed above?

Starting a group

It is quite likely that, at some time during your career, you will decide to start a group related to your work. It could be a support group for parents, or perhaps one for volunteers. Or you might want a group of people to collaborate on a specific task such as planning a programme of in-service training to meet their own working needs.

Meeting place

The room you meet in should be reasonably comfortable, so that people feel at ease and not distracted by such things as hard chairs, draughts coming under the door, or noise.

There should be an understanding that other people will not come in and out during the meeting. This is especially important for a support group. The meeting place should be for that group only for the course of their meeting, otherwise it is difficult to achieve an atmosphere of trust and it is more difficult to concentrate.

The meeting room should not be so large that the group is like a small island in the middle of a large sea of space. This is intimidating and makes communicating with others more difficult. If you have to use a large hall, think about making one half into your meeting place, using a screen, if one is available, to mark off the space.

Seating

Arrange the seating so that every person can see everyone else and so can communicate easily with each other. Placing the chairs in a circle is the easiest way to achieve this and is a way of indicating that everyone in the group is of equal value. If you can avoid it do not have a chair squeezed out, outside the circle. A shy person sitting outside the circle may find it difficult to make a contribution.

Putting chairs in rows, with a leader facing them suggests that there is one expert and others who need to learn from him or her. This is not appropriate for many groups, although it may be acceptable in some types of training situations.

First meetings

Prepare your own programme for the first meeting with a welcome and a short statement about why you have invited people to come.

Make sure that people have an opportunity to be introduced and to get to know one another. Even if you know everyone present it is possible that they do not all know one another. One way of doing this is to invite them to introduce themselves around the circle. Or ask them to stand up and find people they do not already know and introduce themselves.

Next help the group to be clear about what they want of the group and why they have come. This can be done by talking to each other in pairs, which helps to break the ice as well as letting group members get to know at least one other person better. Ask people to choose a partner they do not know very well. Ask them to interview each other, finding out: who they are, why they have come, what they are hoping for and if they have questions about why the meeting was called. Tell them they can have about five minutes each. Then in the whole group each person introduces their partner to the others and says what their partner wants from the group and if there is anything they are still unsure about. (It can feel safer to speak about somebody else than about oneself.) This exercise places all the different expectations and queries out into the open, for the whole group to hear.

Come to agreement about what is a realistic goal for the group. You may want to write it up on a large piece of paper. Also decide about how the meetings are to be run – will you have one leader or will you take it in turns to lead? How many meetings do you think you will need? Where will they be held and when? How long will each meeting last? Knowing these details in advance helps people to feel confident about a group.

Being a leader

The job of the leader is to be of service to the group and to see that it fulfils its purpose. Good leaders let the group have a life of its own. They do not make decisions for the group, but let decisions come from the group. They do not talk too much but they are always alert and observant. They try to be aware of the group atmosphere and of the feelings of individual members. They are in touch with whether the group is fulfilling its purpose, or not, and can express this for the group. Leading a group is not always easy, but drawing on your own interpersonal skills helps, as does experience.

Let the group's purpose be clear

You need to help the group to be aware of what its purpose is by reminding them of earlier agreements. At some point they may need to clarify their purpose again. Members may ask for this directly or indirectly. For example, you may notice that different group members seem to have somewhat different ideas about the group's aim. Or someone may say something like 'What is this meeting about? I think we're missing the point.' If this happens the group needs to spend a little time on clarifying and reaching agreement. Make sure, however, that continual talking about aims is not just a way of avoiding the real work of the group.

Provide a structure for the meeting

Groups can feel insecure if they do not know how a session will be structured. So always introduce the subject of the meeting and say how it is going to be approached. Here are some more points which may be useful:

- In the case of support groups, agree in advance that whatever is spoken about in the meeting will be confidential and not raised outside the group. (If any problems arise because of this – for example if you learn something which suggests that a child may be in real danger – follow the advice given in Chapter 13.)

- You may be using discussion material from outside which will have its own structure. But you may need to adapt it for the group's own needs: are all the discussion points appropriate? Is there enough material…or too much?

- If you are supplying the material for the meeting yourself, say briefly what you are going to do. For example, 'I thought it would be a good idea if we looked through these cuttings I've taken from the local paper, and choose one that seems of most concern to you as a parent. This could start our discussion on what families need in this town.' You would also have ready

155

some questions which could encourage people to share their experience and insights with each other. Open questions are more useful than closed questions to achieve this (see p.92).

- Some groups need to reach decisions about a task which they have undertaken. The decisions should be outlined as an introduction to the meeting. 'We need to choose a volunteer to represent us on the community council and we need to outline the most important things for them to say on our behalf.' If there are many decisions to be made, then a written agenda – either as a handout or written up on a large sheet of paper – will keep everybody informed about what is to be done.

- It is also your job, as leader, to assist the group in deciding whether they want to follow any 'side track' which is beginning to take up group time. This might mean leaving the agreed subject of the meeting for a later date. Unless a group actually makes a decision about this, for or against, problems arise and members feel frustrated. If the 'side track' is lengthy they may not achieve what they set out to achieve by the end of the meeting. On the other hand, if the new material is not discussed, some group members may believe that unforeseen and important issues have been ignored. So let the group come to their own decision about this. Point out any implications of the decision such as that the subject that was previously agreed for discussion needs to be dealt with at a later date.

- Sum up for the group at the end of a session. Remind them of any decisions taken, or briefly acknowledge the explorations and discoveries that have been made.

- Set the date for the next meeting.

- Be the time-keeper for the meeting and see that it begins and ends promptly. This is most important. If meetings start late, tasks may not be completed and people may come later and later for each meeting. At the end of a meeting, people who are kept beyond a stated time can become distracted, thinking of their other commitments (such as getting back for a baby-sitter) or they may have to leave early – and miss information (like the date of the next meeting). Keeping to the agreed time can help people to feel secure in a group.

Help to keep communication flowing

- As leader, listen carefully to each person's contribution.
- If people look puzzled, check where the difficulties lie and get members to clarify any misunderstandings.
- Encourage people who have difficulty in expressing their thoughts or feelings, by reflecting back (see p.65).
- Notice if someone is trying to get into the discussion and help them to do so, if necessary: 'Bernard, you wanted to say something...'
- Help people to work through disagreements, aiming at solutions which are good for both sides (see p.126).
- Bring up new points, or ask open questions (see p.92), if the group needs to be moved along.

When it's time for the group to close

It is sometimes necessary for groups to decide if they want to continue or to continue in the same way. It is not valuable to carry on if people are becoming dispirited and confused or if their work is finished. There are various options available.

When members move away, or leave for other reasons, the group can decide to recruit new people. They should realise, however, that new members will bring different resources, experiences and needs. If there are many new members it will probably be necessary to work together on a restatement of the group's purpose.

Sometimes people feel that their original purpose has been achieved and in this case they should decide if they want to set new goals. If they are no longer sure why they are meeting, they need to take time to look at their original purpose and to decide if they want to move on from it or to return to it.

It is also possible to decide that the group has come to the end of its useful life and that no purpose is served by continuing. If this is so then farewells should be said, either quietly or with a party!

Communicating in groups and meetings: key points

- Groups of all sorts are part of social life. Bringing people together in groups and meetings can encourage creativity and pool skills and experience.

- Each member of a group should take responsibility for its effective functioning; it is not just the business of the leader.

- There are different sorts of groups for different tasks, and different types of group leadership. Directive leaders are seen as experts who tell others how to carry out tasks – sometimes an appropriate style but rarely applying in the context of this book. Facilitative leaders assist members of mutual support groups to define and explore their own interests. In collaborative working groups, the joint attention of the chairperson and of group members is on carrying out agreed tasks, using all the expertise which is in the group.

- Members of sharing and collaborative groups (and staff meetings, where the two types of group can overlap) should be responsible for making whatever contribution is in their power. They should use concrete examples and avoid jargon and unnecessary theory. They should be aware of their feelings and willing, on occasion, to express them.

- They should be sensitive towards other group members, let them into the discussion and encourage their communications. They should also be prepared to confront other individuals if necessary.

- Groups can use many ways to avoid carrying out their task. Some groups get side-tracked onto subjects which are not to the point. Or a scapegoat may be blamed for group failures. Avoiding group responsibilities in this way should be challenged by group members who become aware of it.

- Starting a new group means making decisions about a comfortable meeting place where the group is unlikely to be disturbed. The person who has called the group together should make the reason for doing so clear.

- A group leader should take care about introducing group members to each other, facilitate members' contributions to group discussion and work, and keep the group on task.

- A time comes when a group should either decide to disband or redefine its purpose.

CHAPTER 13

Confidentiality

Confidentiality is the last subject in *Communication Skills for Working with Children and Young People*, but it is far from the least important. Social pedagogy is an ethical practice. It involves considering situations in terms of professional responsibilities and sometimes taking hard decisions. This is especially relevant in the area of confidentiality. This chapter covers aspects of confidentiality that you are likely to meet in your dealings with adults and children at work, how you treat information which is disclosed to you and whether, as a professional responsibility, you pass it on to someone else or not. The chapter does not cover subjects like storing sensitive written information or who has access to written or computerised records. These are significant matters but they do not come under the heading of interpersonal communications.

Private information can be passed on to you in different ways; here are two of them.

Parents confide in you

In the course of your work, especially if you get on well with people, you will find that parents confide in you and tell you about their worries and problems. This may be because they like you and find you trustworthy, which is quite likely to happen if you treat them with sensitivity and respect. But, quite apart from their feelings about you, they may also need to confide in you just because of the job you do. They confide in you first and foremost because you are a professional working with their child. They might tell you private family details so that you can understand their child better. For example:

> You tell a father, when he comes to pick up his toddler, that she's not her usual self; she is being a bit whiny and clinging.

He explains that her mother is suffering from depression and has been taken into hospital. He did not tell you earlier because, he says, 'People can be funny about mental illness.'

This father would of course expect you to treat what he has told you as confidential. He has let you know about his problem because you work with his child, and need to understand her. He would not have told you otherwise.

Senior staff pass on private information

Senior staff also may give you private information about families – not because it is interesting but so that you can do your job properly. For example:

> Social workers have had concerns about Cathie, a child who has been physically abused by her mother's boyfriend who is now under police investigation. They disclose their concerns to the head of the nursery where she has been found a place. They do so because nursery staff need to be aware of any unexplained bumps or bruises which might be a sign of further abuse and which they would have to bring to the attention of the social worker involved in the case. In turn, the head of the nurseries explains Cathie's background to the senior staff who will work with her every day.

Being trustworthy

When someone, parents or colleagues, discloses private information about children and families obviously you do not gossip about it. It takes little imagination to understand how hurtful it would be for your own private business to be discussed by other people and so you extend the same respect to others. In everyday life some people find it exciting to receive private information and to be able to pass it on and see the effect it has on their audience. But people who work with children should think of themselves as professionals who do not divulge confidential matters to third parties.

Gossiping is unprofessional: it doesn't respect the right to keep personal matters private

Passing on information

At the same time it is sometimes professionally necessary to discuss private matters which you have been told about in the course of your work. If you need to do this (we look at the reasons later) you should go to a senior staff member or, in the case of people working alone, directly to children's social services.

- In hospital a nursery nurse should go to the ward sister.
- Playworkers should approach the senior play worker.
- In a young people's residential home staff should go to the manager.
- A nursery officer should go to the officer-in-charge.
- In a school, staff should confide in the head teacher.
- Foster carers and childminders should get in touch with children's social services.
- Staff in the voluntary sector would go to their line manager.

Talking to senior staff about any information which causes you concern, because of possible consequences for a child or young person, is not the same as gossiping. Sometimes it is necessary to pass on private information to colleagues for the sake of a child – just as the social worker, in the example given above, told the nursery manager about the child who had suffered physical abuse. Although the necessity to pass on private information may occur very rarely, it is something that all staff should be prepared for.

'Need to know'

There are useful ground rules for deciding when to pass on information about a child, or a family, to other colleagues. Decisions should be made on the basis of whether other staff need to know. Answering the following questions should clarify whether or not it is necessary to inform colleagues about confidential material.

- Is this knowledge essential for colleagues to work effectively with the child or offer a satisfactory service to the family?

- Are there dangers for the child or the family if this information is not passed on to other members of staff?

If the answer to either question is 'yes', then the information should be passed on to all those who need it professionally. People in a junior position should tell whoever is in charge, who will then decide if the matter should go any further. If you are ever given information by a parent that worries or upsets you it is your duty to discuss it, in confidence, with your manager.

Some services such as day nurseries or young people's residential homes have a system of 'key workers' by which one person is especially responsible for liaising with families and is seen as the person who needs to know the relevant information about the family. In other services all staff who ever work directly with the child or young person concerned are given necessary information. This could include all those who 'cover', that is act as substitutes, for people who usually work with the child. Decisions about this are made by senior staff. For example:

> There is a court order which does not allow Linda's father to have access to her. Linda's mother tells the member of staff in charge of the holiday playscheme that in no circumstances is Linda to be allowed to leave with her father. The senior playworker lets the other two staff know about this, because it is possible that she herself might not be present if the

father turned up and the other staff might, unsuspectingly, hand Linda over to him.

Reflection: things to discuss or think about

- Do you think that it is acceptable for practitioners to discuss private information about families in any of the following circumstances: in case conferences; at home; over coffee in the staff room; in staff meetings; in discussions during training courses?
- Can you think of any exceptions to the answers you've given?

Dangers in passing on private information

As well as advantages, there are also dangers in passing on information. These include, first and foremost, infringing the privacy of the family concerned: it cannot be stated too strongly or too often that families have a right to privacy and infringing it should only happen in the real interests of the child.

Secondly, there is no reason why staff should be burdened with unnecessary details about the families they work with. Some services take children whose families are in extremely difficult circumstances - but knowing all the details of the children's backgrounds would be of little help to the staff concerned. Taking the example of Cathie, given above (see p.161); the children's social service department expect staff to be alert to any signs of injury. It is, therefore, necessary for them to know Cathie's background, so that they do not dismiss any bruising, or other damage, lightly. But there is no need for staff to be told other sensitive material about the family, which could both distress them and prejudice their relationship with the family.

So if a mother confides about her own unhappy childhood, there is no need for you to pass the information on. It has nothing to do with how you look after her child and no danger will arise because other staff have not been informed. But, once again, if you find that a confidence is upsetting or worrying, you should tell your line manager about it. In these circumstances you should be able to look to them for professional support and to make any decisions about further disclosure that are necessary.

Declare you are going to pass information on

If you decide that what you have been told should be made known to others, then you should say so to the person who has confided in you, or who has made disclosures to you or others in a group meeting. For example:

> Deidre is a mother of a child in the class where you are a teaching assistant. You get on well with her. She tells you that her sister's children, also in your class, are left alone for hours every night while their mother is working at a local pub. Deidre has heard them crying as she passes the house. She has spoken to her sister about it but her sister says that there is nothing she can do – the family needs the money. Deidre says 'Please don't say anything, I don't want to cause trouble, but I'm worried sick about it.'

This is a difficult position for you to be in, and the sort of situation which could arise in other settings, also. On the one hand you believe that there is real danger for the children, on the other you feel loyalty towards Deidre who has confided in you. In a situation like this, where children are at risk, you have no option but to pass the information on to your line manager. But you must tell the person who has confided in you that you are going to do so, otherwise they are in a false position. They may believe that you are relating to them in a purely personal way, as a friend, while for you professional responsibilities towards the children have priority. Explain that you know it is very difficult for them but that, for the sake of the children, you are going to tell your own line manager about your concerns for the children. If you are working as a childminder the person to inform would be a member of staff in children's social services.

Reflection: things to discuss or think about

Read the following cases and, with a partner or in small groups if possible, decide what you would do. Read over the key points which follow to help you to come to your answer. There may not be one 'right' answer, you will probably be able to think of different circumstances which would affect what you would do.

1. Saleem is a three-year-old at nursery school. One morning, when you are looking at his painting, he says 'My mum shouted at my dad and she's gone away now.' How do you react? Do you report it to anyone or not? Should you, or a senior worker, 'check out' if what Saleem says is true? What are your reasons for your course of action?

2. A mother, who has a new baby, brings her older child to the holiday club. She is weeping and says she doesn't know what to do. She says she is having problems feeding her new baby and that she suffered severe depression after the birth of her first baby. What do you do, if anything, about this information? Why?

3. You work in residential care. During a phone call about Mason's next visit home, his mother tells you that his father is HIV positive. To whom – if anyone – do you pass this information on? On what grounds do you make this decision?

4. You do a home visit to a family where the child, Tom, has just started nursery class. Tom's mother tells you, in confidence, that his father often beats him. What do you say to her and what action, if any, do you take?

Confidentiality: key points

- Staff are sometimes given sensitive information concerning the families they work with. This information should not be talked about to other parents, nor to anyone who is not professionally concerned with the child or the family.

- Passing on information infringes the privacy of the people concerned. It can also be a burden for colleagues and one which, in some cases, prejudices staff against a family.

- Sensitive information should be passed on to other colleagues only if they need to know and it is in the child's best interests.

- If you have any worries about information you have received, speak to your line manager, who will then take responsibility for who else, if anyone, should know.

- If you decide that you are going to talk to a senior colleague about a parent's private affairs, you must let the parent know you are going to do this, as part of your professional duty.

CHAPTER 14

Interpersonal Communication in Children's Services

Overview

This last short chapter takes an overview of interpersonal communication in terms of social pedagogy, highlighting some of the main themes and ideas covered in this book. A Bibliography follows the chapter with suggestions for more advanced study.

In social pedagogy, effective interpersonal communications are those which best serve children and young people, as individuals and as members of society. The book has suggested ways in which you can develop interpersonal skills which are, first and foremost, used in their interests. This holds for face-to-face communication with children and young people themselves and for all the interactions with adults, parents and colleagues which directly affect them.

You can use the skills described in the preceding chapters with adults and children to:

- *Listen.* Other people have a right to be heard. Listening shows respect and builds self-esteem. A willingness to listen, and knowing how to do so, is fundamental to effective interpersonal communication and the basis for building good relationships. Social pedagogy is based in relationships that are both personal and professional.

- *Avoid interference.* If you have done the observations and exercises described in this book, you are becoming aware of what interferes with effective communication, especially the part that feelings play in distorting communication. If what you have to say is not based in respect, the other person may pay more attention to that part of your message and their emotional reaction to it, and block out the rest.

- *Reflect back.* You have learned that it is effective to 'reflect back' to let people know that you have heard what they have said and understand their feelings. Reflecting back lets them know that you accept their experience – their 'life world' – which is different from your own, and can encourage them to express themselves.

- *Use questions with discrimination.* You understand the difference between different sorts of questions and you have learned something about answering children's and young people's questions carefully. The chapter on questions indicated some of the problems if you ask too many questions or ask pointless questions. Answering children's questions fruitfully depends on being attentive to them and taking what puzzles them seriously – dialogue is important.

- *Speak to people about unacceptable behaviour, without challenging their self-esteem.* The exercises in Chapters 10 and 11 have provided practice in how to confront the behaviour, rather than the person: this can be crucial for people's self-respect.

Effective communicators can take the other person's point of view. It is an essential interpersonal skill to be able to take the other person's point of view: to listen carefully to what they have to say and to be aware of their non-verbal communications. If you are alert to the many different messages an adult or child is sending, you are in a better position to respond to them. You can, for example, spot that someone is upset – although they do not tell you in so many words – and take this into account in how you respond.

Taking the other person's point of view is necessary in interactions with babies, as well as with adults and older children. From the beginning babies are individuals with their own experiences and wishes – even if they do not have the ability to put these into words. With babies you need to be sensitive to how they are at any one moment. Are they sleepy, fretful, alert or crying, for example? What information do they give about whether they are enjoying a game and ready for it to be developed further, or want it to stop? Often they take the lead and engage you in play and interaction – but you have to be alert to their signals, to be able to see things from their point of view. If you are, then you know when they are ready for you to take your 'turn' to play, and can time your contribution so that it fits in.

Effective communicators are aware of the part that feelings play in interpersonal communications. Your own and the other person's feelings play a part in all interpersonal communications. If you learn to pay attention to another person's feelings you can understand their 'messages' more completely. If you become more aware of your own feelings, you are less likely to let them *interfere* with what another person is trying to get across to you.

Effective communicators respect other people. Respect is shown in many ways, but at its heart is a recognition that other people have an individual experience of life, that they have their own feelings and ways of understanding and they have the right to be treated equally. This can be shown by trying to understand the other person's point of view and letting them know that you are doing so: that is acknowledging their experience, not dismissing or ignoring it. It may be more difficult to do this with some people than with others – it is not possible to *like* people equally. But, as a professional, it is important to take your share of responsibility for making relationships work. So when there are conflicting interests, you try to find ways which meet other people's needs as well as your own; you do not try to control them with blame or judgemental language.

Respect is also shown in how you deal with confidential material. You respect people's right to privacy and only breach confidentiality if a child is in danger – and you tell your informant that you are going to do so.

Similarly, it is a spirit of respect which leads you to avoid *stereotyping* other people or giving other messages of power and control which keep other people 'in their place' – such a place is always an unequal one. Giving respect to all the people you work with promotes equality for all groups, including those who are oppressed by racism, sexism, disablist practices and other systematic injustice.

In conclusion, interpersonal communication is going to play an important part in your working life. The skills introduced in *Communication Skills for Working with Children and Young People,* and understandings of the richness which social pedagogy has to offer, can be developed throughout your career. They are skills and understandings which will be of service to parents, to colleagues and, above all to the many children and young people for whose well-being – physical, intellectual, social and emotional – you will share responsibility.

Bibliography

Barnett Pearce, W. (2007) *Making Social Worlds: A Communication Perspective*. Oxford: Blackwell Publishing.

Fawcett, M. (2009) *Learning Through Child Observation*. London: Jessica Kingsley Publishers.

Foley. P. and Leverett. S. (eds) (2008) *Connecting with Children: Developing Working Relationships*. Bristol: Policy Press.

Foley, P. and Leverett, S. (eds) (2010) *Children and Young People's Spaces: Developing Practice*. Basingstoke: Palgrave Macmillan.

Gaine, C. (ed.) (2010) *Equality and Diversity in Social Work Practice*. Exeter: Learning Matters.

Hargie, O.D.W. (2010) *Skilled Interpersonal Communication: Research, Theory and practice*. London: Routledge.

Koprowska, J. (2010) *Communication and Interpersonal Skills in Social Work*. 3rd edn. Exeter: Learning Matters.

Murray, L. and Andrews, L. (2000) *The Social Baby*. Richmond: CP Publishing.

Nelson-Jones, R. (1996) *Relating Skills*. London: Cassell.

Petrie, P. (1994) *Care and Play, Out of School*. London: HMSO.

Petrie, P., Boddy, J. Cameron, C., Wigfall, V. and Simon, A. (2006) *Working with Children in Care: European Perspectives*. Buckinghamshire: Open University Press.

Petrie P. (2011) 'Interpersonal Communication: The Medium for Social Pedagogic Practice.' In C. Cameron and P. Moss (eds) *Social Pedagogy and Working with Children and Young People: Where Care and Education Meet*. London: Jessica Kingsley Publications.

Pinney, R (1984) *Bobby – Breakthrough of an Autistic Child*. 2nd edn. London: Harvill Press.

Schaffer, H.R. (2003) 'Social Interaction and the Beginnings of Communication.' In A. Slater and G. Bremner (eds) *An Introduction to Developmental Psychology*. Oxford: Blackwell.

Tizard, B. and Hughes, M. (2002) *Young Children Learning*. Chichester: Blackwell Publishing.

In the UK, the field of social pedagogy is constantly changing, and the best way to keep up to date with developments is to join mailing lists and visit websites including:

www.infed.org/biblio/b-socped.htm

www.socialpedagogyuk.com/

www.socialpedagogy.co.uk/index.htm

www.unicef.org.uk

Index

Index

Lightning Source UK Ltd.
Milton Keynes UK
UKOW06f2309310516

275372UK00001B/33/P